INSTANT CREDIT REPAIR KIT

How To Do Your Own Credit Repair

Instant Credit Repair Kit: How To Do Your Own Credit Repair

ISBN

1-884350-85-2

NOTICE:This publication is designed to provide valuable information. It is sold with the understanding that the publisher or author is not engaged in rendering legal, accounting, or other professional service. If legal advise or other assistance is required, the service of a competent professional should be sought.

The author and publishers disclaim any personal loss or liability caused by utilization of any information presented in this book. Claims of liability, if any, shall be limited to the amount paid for the book.

INSTANT CREDIT REPAIR KIT

Table of Contents

Introduction

If it wasn't for bad credit,
I'd have no credit at all

Anonymous

If you believe the ads you see on TV, hear on the radio and read in the newspaper, having bad credit is no big deal. Someone promises quick, easy financing, even if you've had a bankruptcy. Well, if that were true, bad credit — even no credit - certainly wouldn't be a problem. But, unfortunately, the ads aren't true. Your credit rating does matter.

Just read the fine print on those "easy credit" ads. People with bad credit and bankruptcies are paying double, triple or even quadruple the amount of interest that an individual with good credit pays. For example, right now, if your credit is good, you can buy a brand new car for 0% financing — that's no interest at all. That means you can be behind the wheel of a brand new Ford Explorer for around $466 a month. On the other hand, if your credit is shall we say somewhat less-than-perfect, you'll likely pay an interest rate anywhere from 18% to 20% . That same Ford Explorer would cost you nearly $696 a month, or an additional $13,750.80 over the life of a five year loan.

Besides paying less for the things you want, like a new car or a new house, there are many other benefits to having good credit. Consider the following:

* More employers than ever before are checking the credit histories of

prospective employees. If your credit is good enough, you'll have an edge on competitors who haven't proven to be as financially responsible as you.

* If you apply for certain types of insurance, most insurance companies will automatically check your credit report. Having good credit can qualify you for the best rates.

* Having good credit also makes it much easier for you to obtain more credit whenever you need it at the lowest possible rates.

So, the question is, "just how good is your credit?"

If your answer you answer is "bad", "need's some repair", or "I don't know", the Instant Credit Repair Kit is designed just for you.

On the following pages we'll provide information about the three major credit reporting agencies and how, by virtue of compiling and maintaining your credit report in a single file, they actually control your financial future. That may be a bold statement, but considering the fact that even if you have never missed a payment, and you think your credit rating should be perfect, your credit report, maintained by the three big boys in the credit reporting industry, could very well say otherwise.

The hard truth is that errors in your credit report could mean that you will be forced to borrow at the highest interest rates offered, or not be given new credit at all. And all through no fault of your own.

In chapter 1, will tell you who the 3 major players in the credit reporting industry are and how they wield such power. You'll also learn the good news — the power you have as a consumer, backed by federal law to fight back and clear your credit record of errors and inaccuracies that can keep you from getting credit.

Chapter 2 provides the information you need to obtain a copy (possibly free) of your credit report from the big three credit reporting agencies, and then how to read and understand the report so you can find any errors it might contain.

In chapter 3 you'll find a step-by-step guide for disputing and correcting errors in your credit report, and how to take advantage of your credit rights under the Fair Credit Reporting Act and other federal and state laws.

We've also included 20 different pre-written letters - everything you'll need, from disputing errors in your credit report to "opting-out" of mailing lists. There's also a Credit Information Dispute form, just ready for you to fill in the blanks and send to each of the three major credit reporting agencies.

This edition of the Instant Credit Repair Kit also includes chapters providing guides for how to deal with debt, avoid the proliferation of credit-related scams that could seriously damage your credit rating, how to protect your credit and financial privacy, and how to maintain a good credit rating so you can always get the credit you need, when you need it.

And now, before you begin, you should understand that nothing on the following pages is intended to serve as legal advice. What we have provided in the Instant Credit Repair Kit is an overview of the credit reporting industry — what it is and how it can adversely affect your credit, through no fault of your own. We've also provided an explanation of your rights, under federal law, for getting a copy of your credit record and the power you have to force the bureaus into correcting mistakes and inaccuracies that damage your credit rating. You can read the full text of several of the most important federal laws, including the Fair Credit Reporting Act in the Appendix of this book.

One more caveat before you begin learning how to repair and then maintain your good credit: The information provided in this book is accurate as of the time of publication. However, federal and state legislation is constantly changing. Check your local library, newspapers or the Internet for the most current information on laws that affect your consumer credit rights.

Chapter 1

Understanding Credit Reporting Agencies

> In this world, nothing is certain but death and taxes... and Credit. Benjamin Franklin - as amended for the 21st

If Benjamin Franklin were alive today, he might very well add one more certainty to his famous "death and taxes" quotation. For in today's world, credit, like death and taxes, is inescapable.

The American economy is based on credit. That's because few of us have enough cash on hand or even in the bank to purchase many of the big ticket items that are "essential" to everyday life. Having access to credit allows you to acquire and enjoy such major assets as a car, house or a college education. Even your ability to obtain medication and medical treatment may very well depend on your access to credit. In addition, significant changes in your life, such as divorce, loss of income, relocation, retirement, and loss of a spouse, may all trigger a need for you to obtain credit, or to review your current credit report.

Maintaining a good credit history and establishing good sources of credit are an essential part of your financial well-being. While lenders consider a number of factors when deciding whether or not to give you credit. Most of them rely heavily on your credit history, which can be found in your credit report. So, building and maintaining a good credit history is essential if you want to continue to get credit or borrow money.

Simply put, your credit history, which is on file at credit reporting agencies, reflects your entire financial life on paper. It contains your Social Security number, current and past addresses, employment, loans, credit cards, mortgages and all other debts. It shows your payment history, whether you've filed for bankruptcy within the past ten years and other information creditors use in determining whether or not to give you credit and how much to give you. Credit reporting agencies collect this information from merchants, lenders, landlords, etc., and then sell the report to creditors so that they can evaluate your application for credit. Obviously, if the information complied by credit reporting agencies is incorrect or incomplete your application for credit could run into serious trouble.

Credit Reporting Agencies

Credit reporting agencies (CRA), also called credit bureaus, are the backbone of the multi-billion dollar credit reporting industry. According to the Consumer Data Industry Association (CDIA), — formerly the Associated Credit Bureau, Inc. — an international trade association representing CRAs, mortgage reporting companies, and collection service companies in the United States, there are nearly 650 credit reporting agencies in the United States, 500 of which are CDIA members. Most of these CRAs are either owned or otherwise affiliated with one of the three big boys, which rule the credit reporting industry: Equifax, Experian, and TransUnion. Each of the "big three" companies maintain 190 million credit files, called credit reports, which are used by the smaller, independent CRAs across the country. In the credit industry, all roads lead to Equifax, Experian and TransUnion.

To better understand the power wielded by credit reporting agencies — specifically the big three — in determining your access to credit, it's important to have at least a basic understanding of how these agencies work.

If you've ever applied for credit, perhaps for a charge account, a personal loan, insurance, and so on, there is a file on you. In that file is information about where you work and live, how you pay your bills, and whether you've been sued, arrested, or filed for bankruptcy. CRAs are companies that gather and sell that information in the form of consumer or credit reports to creditors, employers, insurers, and other businesses. But, you shouldn't feel singled out. It isn't just your life these CRAs are keeping track of. There currently are one billion credit cards in use in the United States. A similar number of consumer reports are issued in the U.S. every year. And two billion pieces of data are entered monthly into consumers' credit records.

Businesses inspect your credit history when they evaluate your application for credit, insurance, employment, and even leases. Based on your credit payment history, business can choose to grant or deny you credit, provided you receive fair and equal treatment. Bad credit, which is a reflection of the information in your credit report, can affect your ability to get more credit. It also can affect your ability to get or keep a job. Employers often use a credit report when they hire and evaluate employees for promotion, reassignment or retention.

Your Credit Report

Contrary to popular belief, CRAs do not keep track of every aspect of your personal life. CRAs simply gather and sell four basic types of information:

1) Identification and employment data: This may include you name, birth date, address, Social Security number, employer and spouse's name. A CRA also may provide other information, such as your employment history, home ownership, income, and previous address, if a creditor asks for it.

2) Payment history: This information lists your account record with various creditors, showing how much credit has been extended to you and how you have repaid it. It may include late payments reported by utility companies, landlords, and hospitals, as well as overdrawn accounts reported by banks. Late credit card, auto loan, and mortgage payments reported by banks also may be recorded in your file.

3) Inquiries: CRAs are required to keep records of all creditors who have requested your credit report within the past six months. They usually keep such creditor inquiries in your file for at least six months.

4) Public record information: This includes events that are a matter of public record and are directly related to your "credit worthiness", such as bankruptcy, foreclosures, delinquent child support payments, and tax liens.

What's Not In Your Report

* Your race

* Your religion

* Your current health or medical history

* Your driving record

* Your political preference

* Notice of bankruptcy that is more than 10 years old

* Debts that are more than 7 years old.

Who Can Access Your Credit Report?

The federal Fair Credit Reporting Act (FCRA), which we discuss later in this chapter, and individual state laws restrict who has access to the sensitive and personal information in your credit file, and how it may be used. According to the FCRA, access to your credit report is limited to the following:

* Potential lenders may view consumer credit reports to help them decide whether or not to extend credit, to review an account, or to collect a debt.

* Employers and potential employers may access your file (usually only with your written consent). This information is made available to help employers make decisions about hiring, firing, promotion or reassignment.

* Insurance companies may see your credit report to access information that will help them in underwriting a personal, automobile, family, household or medical insurance policy.

* Any government agency may review credit reports for the purposes of granting credit, hiring or insuring.

* Entities considering your application for a government license or benefit (if the agency must consider your financial status).

* Companies with which you have a credit account may review your credit report for account monitoring purposes.

* A state or local child support enforcement agency. Such an agency can review credit files to help it determine whether or not a parent must pay child support, and if so, the amount of the payments.

* Legitimate business needs. Your record may be reviewed in connection with a business transaction you initiate, which may include the purchase of goods or services for your personal, family or household use.

The Fair Credit Reporting Act

The Federal Trade Commission enforces credit laws that protect consumer rights to obtain, use and maintain credit. One such law, the Fair Credit Reporting Act (FCRA) is specifically designed to promote accuracy and ensure the privacy of the information used in consumer reports. Recent amendments to the Act expand consumer rights and place additional requirements on CRAs. Business that supply information about you to CRAs and those that use consumer reports also have new responsibilities under the FCRA.

Among other things, the FCRA says that you must be told what's in your credit report and have any errors corrected. That's important to remember, especially since mistakes on your credit record can cast a cloud over your credit future. By exercising your rights under the FCRA, you can ensure that your CRA records are both complete and accurate.

If a lender refuses you credit because of unfavorable information in your credit report, the FCRA gives you the right to get the name and address of the agency that keeps your report. Then, you may either request information from the CRA by mail or in person (see Chapter 2 for detailed information on how to obtain a copy of your credit report). While you may not get an exact copy of the file, you will at least learn what's in your report. If you're questioning a credit refusal made within the past 60 days, the CRA is not allowed to charge a fee for giving you the information.

When you notify a CRA about an error in your report, the FCRA requires that the credit reporting agency investigate and resolve the dispute within 30 days after receiving your notice. The CRA must contact the creditor who supplied the data and remove any information that is incomplete or inaccurate from your credit report. If you disagree with the findings, the FCRA gives you the right to file a short statement (100 words) in your report, presenting your side of the story. All future reports to creditors must include this statement or a summary of it.

The FCRA also gives consumers a number of other important rights. Listed below is a summary of those rights. The complete text of the FCRA can be found in Appendix A, and detailed explanations of the rights granted by this important federal law may be found on the following pages of this book.

Summary of Consumer Rights Under The FCRA

* The right to find out what information is in your credit report. At your request, a CRA is required to provide you with the information in your report, as well as a list of everyone who has requested your report recently. There is no charge for the report if action has been taken against you because of information supplied by a CRA, if you request the report within 60 days of receiving notice of the action. You also are entitled to one free report every year upon request if you verify that (1) you are unemployed and plan to look for work within 60 days; (2) you are on welfare; or (3) Your report is inaccurate due to fraud. Otherwise a CRA may charge you up to nine dollars for a copy of your report.

* The right to know if your credit report has been used against you. Anyone who uses information from a credit reporting agency to take action against you — such as denying an application for credit, employment, or insurance - must tell you, and give you the name, address and phone number of the CRA that provided the information.

* The right to dispute inaccurate information with a CRA. If you inform a CRA that your report contains inaccurate information, the CRA must investigate the items in question (usually within 30 days) by presenting to its information source all relevant evidence you have submitted (Unless your suit is deemed frivolous). The source must then review your evidence and report its findings to the CRA. The CRA also must give you a written report of the investigation and a copy of your report if the investigation results in any change. If the CRA's investigation does not resolve the dispute, you may add a brief statement to your file. Usually, the CRA also must include a summary of your statement in future reports. If an item is deleted or a dispute is filed, you may request that anyone who has recently received your report be notified of the change.

* The right to have inaccurate information in your report corrected or deleted. A CRA must correct or remove inaccurate or unverified information from its files, usually within 30 days after you file a dispute. If you dispute results in any change to your report, the CRA cannot reinsert into your file a disputed item unless the information source verifies its accuracy and completeness. The CRA must also give you a written notice informing you that it has reinserted the item. The notice must include the name, address and phone number of the information source. (The CRA is not required to remove accurate information from your file unless it is outdated or cannot be verified. Outdated data is described as negative information that is more than seven years old; ten years for bankruptcies)

* The right to dispute inaccurate items with the source of the information. If you inform anyone — such as creditor who reports to a CRA - that you dispute an item, they may not then report the information to a CRA without including a notice of your dispute. And after you've notified the source in writing, it may not continue to report the information if it is, in fact, an error.

* The right to have access to your credit report limited. A CRA may provide information about you only to people with a need recognized by the FCRA — usually to consider an application with a creditor, insurer, landlord, or other business.

* The right to have your consent before your report is provided to employers. A CRA may not give out information about you to your employer, or prospective employer, without first getting your written consent. A CRA also may not report medical information about you to creditors, insurers, or employers without your consent.

* The right to have your name excluded from CRA lists for unsolicited credit and insurance offers. Creditors and insurers may use CRA file information as the basis for sending you unsolicited offers of credit or insurance. Such offers must also include a toll-free phone number for you to call and have your name removed from future lists. If you call, you must be kept off the lists for two years. In addition, if you request, complete and return the CRA form provided for this purpose, you must be taken off the lists indefinitely.

* The right to sue FCRA violators. If a CRA violates the FCRA, you may sure them in state or federal court.

Chapter 2

How To Get A Copy Your Credit Report

The first step in repairing your own credit is finding out what information is in your credit file. It's essential that you know what's in your file because businesses use that information to evaluate your applications for credit, insurance, employment, and other purposes allowed by the FCRA. So you need to know whether or not the information in your report is complete and accurate. Depending on your circumstances (or where you live), you may be entitled to receive a free copy of your credit report, or required to pay a nominal fee of under $10 (plus applicable taxes).

If you've been denied credit, insurance or employment because of information provided by a credit reporting agency, the FCRA requires that the company you applied to give you the CRA's name, address, and telephone number. If you contact the agency for a copy of your report within 60 days of receiving a denial notice, the report is free. In addition, you are entitled by law to one free copy of your report each year if you can prove that (1) you're currently unemployed but plan to look for a job within 60 days, (2) you're on welfare, (3) your report is inaccurate because of fraud. Otherwise , a CRA may charge you up to $9.00 for a copy of your report.

Even if you haven't been denied credit, you may wish to find out what information is in your credit file. Some financial advisors suggest that consumers review their credit reports every one or two years to check for inaccuracies or omissions, which could have a negative effect on your ability to get more credit. This is especially important if you're considering making a major purchase, such as buying a new home. Checking in advance on the accuracy of information in your credit report could help speed-up the credit-granting process.

How To Find The CRA That Has Your Report

You can locate the local and/or regional credit bureau that has your credit report by contacting the CRAs listed in the Yellow Pages under "credit" or "credit rating and reporting". Since more than one CRA may have a file on you, we advise contacting each until you have located all the agencies maintaining your file.

In addition, as noted above, anyone who takes action against you in response to a report provided by a CRA, such as denying your application for a loan, insurance or employment, must give you the name, address and telephone number of the CRA that supplied the report.

Contacting The Big Three

There are three ways you can get a copy of your credit report from each of the big three CRAs:

1) Send each a letter, requesting a copy of your credit report.

2) Order your report by phone, using the CRAs credit report request toll-free phone number.

3) Order a copy of your report online, via the Web sites of each of the big Three CRAs.

If ordering by phone or online, you would pay for your credit report with a major credit card.

Listed below are the big three CRAs and how to get a copy of your report from each. While the following information was accurate at the time of publication, it is subject to change. In other words, it's a good idea to call each company's national consumer assistance office for the latest instructions, mailing addresses, etc. If you have access to the Internet, you also may visit each company's Web Site, also listed below.

1) Equifax

Your credit report on file at Equifax contains details on credit cards and loans opened in your name, companies accessing your credit file, payment information and more. The reports costs $9.

* Send a letter requesting a copy of your credit report to:

Equifax Credit Information Services
P.O. Box 740241
Atlanta, GA 30374

* Gain instant online access to your credit report at http://www.equifax.com.

* Order by phone: 1-800-685-1111.

2) Experian

Experian collects and organizes information about consumers and their credit histories from public records, creditors and other "reliable" sources. The cost of the Experian report is $9.

* Send a letter requesting a copy of your credit report to:

Experian

National Consumer Assistance Center
P.O. Box 2002
Allen, TX 75013-09409

* Get instant online access to your credit report at http://www.experian,com.

* Order by phone (toll-free):1-866-200-6020.

3) TransUnion

Fees vary, up to $9.00

* Send a letter requesting a copy of your credit report to:

TransUnion LLC
Consumer Disclosure Center
P.O. Box 1000
Chester, PA 19022

* Instant online access to your credit report is available at http://www.transunion.com.

* Order by phone: At this writing, you can not purchase a copy of your credit report by phone from TransUnion. However, if you meet the criteria for a free credit report (explained earlier in this chapter), you may call 1-800-888-4213 and order your free Credit report from TransUnion.

Writing A Credit Report Request Letter

When requesting a copy of your credit report in writing, you should include very specific identifying information, such as your full name, date of birth, Social Security number (a copy of the front of your Social Security card is preferred), current address, former address (if you haven't been at your current address for at least five years), and the name of your current employer. You also should include your spouse's name, and you phone numbers where you can be reached during the day and at night. Also include proof of identification, such as a copy of your driver's license, a utility bill, billing statement from any major creditor, etc., that reflects your current name and address. And of course, you should be sure to sign the letter, so the CRA has your signature on file. While this may seem like a lot of personal information, it is needed by the CRAs for security purposes.

Keep in mind that if you are writing to a CRA because you have been denied credit, insurance, or employment within the past 60 days because of information about you the CRA has on file, you are entitled to receive a copy of the report at no charge. Just be sure you include with your credit report request, a copy of the notification of credit denial you received from a creditor, insurer, or employer that had access to your credit file.

However, if you just want to do a regular check of your file to review it for inaccuracies and errors, you'll be required to pay a fee. That means along with your credit report request letter, you also need to enclose a check or money order for the appropriate amount.

You also should always send these letters to CRAs through certified and return receipt mail, which is available through your local post office. Once a CRA receives your credit report request letter, it should respond within three business days.

Sample Credit Report Request Letter

January 15, 2002

XYZ Credit Bureau
P.O. Box 000
Anytown, USA 00000

To Whom It May Concern,

Please send me a copy of my current credit report. The following is my current identifying information:

John Q. Citizen
1111 Peaceful Road
Wistful Vista, OH 12121

I have lived at the above address for the past ten years.
My date of birth is 11/25/50.
My Social Security Number is: 111-222-333

I am a self-employed
My daytime phone number is: 111-111-1111

My evening phone number is: 111-222-2222

I have enclosed a check (or money order) in the amount of $9.00 to cover the cost of the report, which may be sent to the above address.

Thank You,

(Your Signature)

Determining How Much Your Report Will Cost

In early January 2002, the Federal Credit Reporting Act increased the fee for a credit report from $8 to $9 (plus any applicable taxes). More than a year later, that maximum fee remains the standard cost for an individual consumer credit report. However, some state laws require free reports or a lesser fee for consumers in their states. And some states also require a tax on consumer credit reports.

At this writing, residents of the following states are entitled to one or more free copies of their credit report each year:

State	First Report	Second Report	Additional Reports
Colorado	Free	$8.00	$8.00
Georgia	Free	Free	$9.00
Maryland	Free	$5.00	$5.00
Massachusetts	Free	$8.00	$8.00
New Jersey	Free	$8.00	$8.00
Vermont	Free	$7.50	$7.50

Residents of the following states, who do not qualify for a free report, must pay the following fee for their credit reports:

State	First Report	Additional Reports
California	$8.00	$8.00
Connecticut	$5.00	$7.50
Maine	$2.00	$2.00
Minnesota	$3.00	$9.00
Montana	$8.50	$8.50
U.S. Virgin Islands	$1.00	$1.00
All Other States	$9.00	$9.00

Remember, besides being denied credit within the last 60 days (as explained earlier in this chapter), you also are entitled to a free copy of your consumer credit report if you are either: 1) unemployed and intend to apply for employment within 60 days; 2) a recipient of public welfare assistance; or 3) have reason to believe that your information on file at a CRA contains inaccurate information due to fraud.

What's In Your Consumer Credit Report

As we touched upon in chapter one, there are four primary categories of information contained in all credit reports:

1) Identifying Information

The following identifying information found in most credit reports, generally is taken from credit and loan applications that you have filled out.

* Your name, including any nicknames you may have used, and whether you are a junior, senior, and so on.

* Your current and previous addresses.

* Your Social security number.

* Your current telephone number.

* Your date of birth.

* Your spouse's name.

* Your current and previous employers.

2) Credit History

This consists of your history of paying bills with creditors, which is reported to the CRAs. And while each credit reporting agency uses its own credit report format, most reports contain the following types of credit history information, as received from retail stores, banks, finance and mortgage companies, and other creditors.

* Names of each creditor and account or loan numbers.

* Type of account or loan - revolving, installment, mortgage, etc.

* Date each accounted was opened.

* Credit limit or loan balance.
* Current balance

* Monthly payment amount and payment pattern over the past several years.

* Amount of credit that has been extended.

* Whether or not a consumer is disputing information related to an account.

3) Public Records

These items which appear in your credit report, generally involve credit-related events that are a matter of public record, such as:

* Tax liens

* Court judgments, including child support payments

* Foreclosures

* Bankruptcies

4) Inquiries

The inquiries section of a credit report generally lists the credit grantors and other authorized parties who have received your credit report. Inquiries also may contain lists of companies that receive your name and address information for the purpose of offering you credit.

How To Read Your Credit Report

Once you've obtained a copy of your credit report, you'll be able to see what your creditors have been saying about you. And you'll most likely be surprised at what you find — not just at the information in your report, but at the information not in your report. It's a rare credit report that has complete information on a consumer's financial history.

Considering that it has been estimated that 50% to 70% of all credit reports in the United States are inaccurate, you need to study your report very carefully. The problem is that credit reports can be somewhat confusing to read.

1) Identifying Information Section

Since this section of your credit report contains identifying information like your name, current address, Social Security number, date of birth, spouse's name (if applicable), etc, it should be a fairly easy read, right? Well, the information is straightforward enough, but the trouble is it may not be accurate. Many people make the mistake of simply skimming over this section, assuming that the information is accurate. Don't make that mistake. Read each entry and make sure everything is correct and up-to-date. Just one piece of inaccurate information in this section and the credit history listed on your report could be wrong.

2) Credit History Section

This is the heart of your credit report so you will want to review it very carefully. It contains a list of your open and past credit accounts and shows any late payments reported by your creditors. If you find any information that is incorrect or accounts that don't belong to you, you'll need to submit a dispute letter to the CRA (see Chapter 3).

Sample Credit Report Credit History Section

Company Name
Account Number
Whose Acct.
Date Opened
Months Reviewed
Last Activity
High Credit
Terms
Balance
Past Due
Status
Sears
12345
I
1/01
24
1/03
3000

R1
Amex
368791
J
12/01
12
12/02
4000

0

O1
FNB
24801
C
1/02
12
1/03
5000
300
4640
300
I2

* Company Name — this identifies the company that is reporting the information.

* Account Number — shows your account number with the company.

* Whose Account — indicates who is responsible for the account and the type of participation you have with the account. Abbreviations in this section may vary depending on the CRA, but some of the most common used are:

> I = Individual
> J = Joint
> U = Undesignated
> A = Authorized User
> M = Maker
> T = Terminated
> C = Co-maker/Co-signer
> S = Shared

* Date Opened — the month and year the account was opened.

* Last Activity — the date of the last activity on the account. This may indicate the date of your last payment or last charge.

* High Credit — indicates your credit limit for each account. If the account is

an installment loan, the original amount will be shown.
* Terms — for revolving accounts (credit cards, etc.), this column usually is left blank; for installment loans, the number of installments may be shown or the amount of the monthly payments.

* Balance — the amount owed on the account at the time it was reported.

* Past Due — indicates any amount past due at the time the information was reported.

* Status — a combination of letters and numbers are used in this column to indicate the type of account and the payment pattern — that is, the timeliness of payment on each account.

Abbreviations used for the type of account are:

> O = Open
> R = Revolving
> I = Installment

Numbers used for timeliness vary among CRAs, but generally are used to indicate how current you are in your payments. Current or "paid as agreed" are typically represented by 0 or 1. Larger numbers — up to nine - indicate that an account is past due.

* Date Reported — shows the last time information on each account was updated by your creditors.

3) Collection Accounts Section

This is the section of your credit report that lists any of your accounts that were referred to a collection agency within the last seven years. The name of the collection agency also will be listed along with the amount you owe and, in some cases, their contact information. If you see a collection listed on your report that doesn't look familiar to you, contact the CRA and submit a dispute letter.

It's also a good idea to contact the collection agency listed in your report to determine the exact nature of the account. You may discover that a collection account listed in your credit report actually belongs to someone whose name or Social Security number is very similar to yours. Believe it or not, that's a common error found on many credit reports. If it happens to you, you should contact the collection agency and provide documented proof that it is not your account, and ask the agency to acknowledge this fact in writing. The collection agency should send you a copy of its letter to you and the credit reporting agency so that the mistake information can be removed from your credit report.

Then again, you also may discover that the collection account is indeed yours. If that's the case, you should determine the accuracy of the amount of the collection account and then make arrangements to pay the amount as soon as possible. Once the collection account has been paid, you should request a letter from the collection agency stating that you have satisfied the obligation in full. In addition, you should make sure that the CRA receives a copy of the letter so that it can list the account in your credit report as paid.

4) Public Records Section

This section also may be referred to as Courthouse Records. It features a listing of public record items (obtained from local, state and federal courts) that reflect your history of meeting financial obligations. This information may include:

* Bankruptcy records
* Tax Liens
* Judgments
* Collection accounts
* Overdue child support (in some states)

Again, you should examine this information carefully. If you find anything that is inaccurate or mistaken, you should contact the CRA and submit a dispute letter.

5) Inquiry Section

The inquiry section of your credit report contains a list of the businesses that have received your credit report within the last 24 months. If you see the names of business that are unfamiliar, you should find out who they are and why they're looking at your credit report. The CRA may be able to provide you with contact information. It's important that you remember only companies that have received your written authorization should be able to check your credit report.

Additional Information

In this section of your credit report, you'll usually find a listing of your former addresses and past employers as reported by your creditors.

Finally, when you review your credit report, you should keep in mind the time information can be retained in your credit file. According to the FCRA:

* Credit and collection accounts will be reported for 7 years from the date of the last activity with the original creditor.

* Chapter 7 or Chapter 11 bankruptcy will be reported for 10 years from the date filed.

* All other courthouse records will be reported for 7 years from the date filed.

Credit Scoring

According to a recent study conducted by the Consumer Federation of America (CFA) and the National Credit Reporting Association (NCRA), millions of Americans could pay more for - or be denied - credit, insurance, or utilities because of inaccurate credit scores. The study, which was conducted in the summer of 2002, analyzed the credit scores of more than 500, 000 consumers, and extensively reviewed the files of more than 1,700 individuals, maintained by the big three CRAs.

And that brings up the next question - what the heck are credit scores? And how do they affect a consumer's credit rating?

While your credit report can be considered your detailed financial history, it isn't the only thing a creditor uses in deciding whether or not you get credit. Creditors also use a credit scoring system, which involves a score that is an objective summary of the information in your credit report. In effect, your credit score represents your creditworthiness as a number.

Actually, it's been going on for years. Creditors have been using credit scoring systems to determine whether or not consumers are good risks for credit cards and auto loans. More recently, creditors have been using a credit scoring system to evaluate consumers' ability to repay home mortgage loans.

Credit scoring is a system wherein information about you and your credit experiences, such as your-bill-paying history, the number and type of accounts you have, late payments, collection actions, outstanding debt and the age of your accounts, is collected from your credit application and your credit report. Using a statistical program, creditors compare this information to the credit performance of consumers with similar credit profiles. The system awards points for each factor that helps predict who is most likely to repay. The total number of points — your credit score — supposedly helps creditors predict whether you're a good credit risk or a bad credit risk. To creditors, your credit score predicts how likely it is that you will repay a loan and make the payments when due. In other words, if your credit score is an important factor in whether or not a creditor decides to grant you credit.

Because your credit report is an important part of most credit scoring systems, you have another good reason to make sure your report is accurate before you submit an application. Otherwise, your credit score could be adversely affected, and as a result, you could be denied credit.

How Credit Scores Are Used

Credit scores are one of the main tools creditors use when determining the risk in lending consumers money. Creditors use scores to decide whether or not to grant you credit and, if so, how much credit and at what rate. Creditors also will access and consider your credit report, which can provide further substantiation on a particular component of a score that could very well affect their final decision. However, since most credit matters are decided very quickly, it is a credit score that is generally the determining factor.

Proponents of the credit scoring system point out that since it is based on real data and statistics, it's usually more reliable than subjective or judgmental methods. It treats all applications objectively — as numbers.

How Is A Credit Score Determined?

Credit scoring systems are complex but generally involve placing numerical weights on different aspects of a credit report and a mathematical formula or computation is used to calculate the final score. To develop a credit scoring model, a creditor chooses a random sample of its customers and analyzes it statistically to identify characteristics that relate to "creditworthiness". Each of these factors is assigned a "weight" based on how strong a predictor it is of who would be a good credit risk.

Each creditor may use its own credit scoring model, different scoring models for different types of credit, or a generic credit scoring model developed by a credit scoring company.
The method most commonly used by lenders is called a FICO, named after its origins with the Fair Isaac and Company. Fair Isaac is an independent company that developed the scoring model and software used by bank and lenders, insurers and other businesses. Each of the three major credit reporting agencies worked with Fair Isaac in the early 1980s to devise this scoring method.

While each of the big three CRAs use their own versions of the FICO score, they all are based on the original Fair Isaac scoring method and produces equivalent numerical results for any given credit report.

The number used to designate your credit score can range from 300 to 900. Here is an approximate example of how a credit score is calculated:

* 35% of the score is based on your payment history.

* 30% of the score is based on outstanding debt.

* 15% of the score is based on the length of time you've had credit.

* 10% is based on the number of inquiries on your report.

* 10% of the score is based on the types of credit you currently have.

How You Can Improve Your Credit Score

Generally, only a creditor can tell you what might improve your score under the particular credit scoring model being used to evaluate your credit. However, scoring models, as you can see from the scoring calculation listed above, generally evaluate the following types of information found in your credit report:

* Whether or not you've paid your bills on time. Payment history almost always is a significant factor in a credit scoring system. It's likely that your score will be affected adversely if you've paid bills late, had an account referred to collections, or declared bankruptcy, if that history appears on your credit report.

* How much outstanding debt you have. Most scoring models evaluate the amount of debt you have compared to your credit limits. If the amount you owe is close to your credit limit that is likely to have a negative effect on your credit score.

* The length of your credit history. Typically, credit scoring models consider the length of your credit history. A relatively short credit track record may have an adverse effect on your score however that can be offset by other factors, such as prompt payments and low balances.

* Whether or not you've applied for new credit recently. Many scoring models consider whether you've applied for credit recently by looking at "inquiries" on your credit report when you apply for credit. If you've applied for too many new accounts recently, that may have a negative effect on your credit score.

* The number and types of credit accounts you have. While it's generally good to have established credit accounts, too many credit card accounts may have a negative effect on your credit score. In addition, many scoring models consider the type of credit accounts you have. For example, under some scoring models, loans from finance companies may have a negative effect on your credit score.

Considering the type of information used in most credit scoring models, the best way to improve your credit score is to make a concerted effort to pay your bills on time, pay down outstanding balances, and don't take on new debt.

Chapter 3

How To Dispute And Correct Credit Report Errors

According to a 1998 study, conducted by the Public Interest Research Group, nearly one third of all consumer credit reports had errors serious enough to cause denial of credit, insurance, housing, employment, etc. However, the Associated Credit Bureaus (now the Consume Data Industry Association) sponsored its own study that reported less than two-tenths of one percent of credit reports contained incorrect information. In reality, the actual percentage is probably somewhere in between those two extremes, but as you can see, the problem does exist and reviewing your credit report for such common errors is a very good idea.

Common Credit Report Errors

The most common credit report errors involve inaccuracies and mixed credit files. Many inaccuracies on a credit report can be the result of simple human error. And that's not too difficult to understand when you consider that the credit reporting industry collects more than two billion pieces of credit-related information every month and generates hundreds of millions of credit reports on nearly 200 million consumers every tear. Given that amount of information to process on that number of consumers, humans are bound to make some mistakes.

- **Mixed Information.** This happens when your credit file includes credit information for someone who has a name similar or identical to yours.

■ **Identifying information is incorrect**. Your name is misspelled, your address is wrong, your Social Security number is wrong, etc.

■ Account information is inaccurate or incomplete. For example, inaccur cies may relate to payments not credited, late payments, etc. Your report also may include incorrect account balances, or report accounts that have been paid off or closed as open.

■ **Outdated information is reported.** Generally, a CRA is required, by law to maintain and report negative account information about a consumer for 7 years and bankruptcy for 10 years.

■ **Unauthorized inquiries are listed.** Whenever you apply for a loan or more credit, creditors check your credit file to help them determine whether or not to give you that credit. Each time a creditor looks at your file, it places an inquiry on your credit report. Inquiries can add up, which often is interpreted as negative by creditors. That's why too many inquiries on your credit report can make getting credit difficult. In addition, if you didn't authorize someone to review your credit report, and they did, they may have broken the law.

■ **Account information that does not relate to you.** This could be the result of identity theft (see Chapter 7, "How To Protect Your Credit And Financial Privacy") and is reason in and of itself to study your credit report carefully. Identity theft is an increasingly more frequent, and insidious crime that involves a thief who assumes your name to open new accounts, divert your credit card statements to another address, and run up a frightening amount of bad debt in your name without you being aware of it until collectors start harassing you. Over time, identity theft could jeopardize your ability to obtain further credit, and cost your thousands of dollars.

The best way to catch such an identity thief is by getting a copy of your credit report, which will show if there are accounts listed that you know you haven't opened.

- **Failure to show that a tax lien has been removed.**

Upon careful review of your credit report, if you discover any of these or other errors, you should attempt to get them corrected as soon as possible. Quick action is important in order to minimize any possible damage to your credit report. And it doesn't matter which CRA provided the credit report with the errors, because the Fair Credit Reporting Act provides a process for disputing and correcting the problem.

Disputing Information In Your Credit Report

Under the FCRA, both the credit reporting agency and the organization that provided the information to the CRA, such as a credit card company, are responsible for correcting inaccurate or incomplete information in your credit report. To take advantage of and protect all your rights under the law, you should contact both the CRA and the information provider whenever you dispute information in your credit report.

Fixing Errors

The first step in the process of correcting errors in your credit report is tell the CRA in writing what information you believe is inaccurate and why. Your letter disputing your credit report also should include copies (not originals) of any documents that support your claim. In addition to providing your complete name and current address, your dispute letter also should clearly identify each item in your report that you believe is inaccurate. Tell them the facts, explain why you dispute the information, and request that the information be deleted or corrected. We also advise including a copy of your report with the information you dispute circled (Your letter may look something like the Sample Letter Disputing A Credit Report shown below). Send your letter by certified mail with a return receipt so you know that it was received. And always keep a record of everything you send, including enclosures.

Next, send a letter to the creditor or merchant who supplied the incorrect information to the CRA, to make it known that you are disputing it. Send copies of the documentation that supports your claim, just as you did with the CRA.

Sample Letter Disputing A Credit Report

Todays Date

Your Name
Your Address
City, State, Zip Code

Name of Credit Reporting Agency
Address
City, State Zip Code

To Whom It May Concern,

I am writing to you to dispute the following information in my credit report. The items I dispute also are circled on the enclosed copy of the report I have received from your agency.

This item (identify item(s) disputed by name of source, such as creditors or tax court, and identify the type of item, such as credit account, judgment, and so on.) is (inaccurate or incomplete) because (describe what is inaccurate or incomplete and why). I am requesting the item be deleted (or request another specific change, such as a correction) as soon as possible.

I have enclosed copies of (if applicable, describe any enclosed documentation, such as payment records, and court documents) which support my position. Please reinvestigate this (these) matter (s) and (delete or correct)the disputed item(s) as soon as possible.

Sincerely
Your Signature

```
Enclosures: (List everything you are enclosing)
```

You also may use the sample “Credit Information Dispute Form” provided in Chapter 8 of this book, to dispute errors in your report.

The CRAs Reinvestigation of Disputed Items

By law, the CRA (any CRA) must reinvestigate the item(s) you question, within 30 days — unless they consider your dispute “frivolous” or “irrelevant”. The also must provide all relevant information you provide about the dispute to the information provider. After the information provider receives notice of a dispute from the CRA, it must investigate, review all relevant information provided by the CRA, and then report the results to the CRA. If the information provider finds that the disputed information is indeed inaccurate, it must notify all nationwide CRAs so that they can correct this information in your credit report.

If, after 30 days from the receipt of your letter of dispute, you haven't heard back from the CRA, you should contact its customer service department. There is usually a toll-free number on the credit report that you can call for assistance. Remember to keep notes of all your conversations and any actions that were taken as a result.

When The Reinvestigation Is Complete

Once the CRA has completed its reinvestigation of the disputed item(s) it must give you the written results and a free copy of your report if your dispute results in any changes. If any information is changed (or deleted) on the report, the CRA cannot change it back unless the information provider supplies proof that it was accurate and the CRA provides you with a written notice that it intends to reinsert the items in your report. Such a written notice also must include the name, address, and phone number of the information provider.

At your request, the CRA must send notices of any correction to anyone who received your report in the past six months. You also can have a corrected copy of your report sent to anyone who received a copy during the past two years for employment purposes.

Using The 100 Word Statement

If the CRA's investigation does not resolve your dispute, the FCRA permits you to file a statement of up to 100 words with the CRA explaining your side of the story. The CRA must include this explanation in your credit report each time it sends it out. If you need help writing your 100 word statement, the FCRA requires that CRAs make employees available to assist you.

Accurate Negative Information In Your Credit Report

If negative information in your credit report is accurate, only the passage of time, as required by the FCRA, can assure its removal. According to the FCRA negative information generally can remain on your credit report for 7 years. The exceptions include:

* Information about criminal convictions may be reported without any time limitations.

* Bankruptcy information may be reported for 10 years.

* Credit information reported in response to an application for a job with a salary of more than $75,000 has no time limit.

* Credit information reported because of an application for more than $150,000 worth of credit or life insurance has no time limit.

* Information about a lawsuit or an unpaid judgment against you can be reported for seven years or until the statute of limitations runs out, whichever is longer.

If you discover that there is negative, but accurate information in your credit report, you can add a 100-word written statement (as described above) to your report, if you believe that the negative information requires an explanation. For example, you may want to explain that your credit history was tarnished because of an unexpected illness or because you lost your job. Your 100-word written statement also should include an explanation of what you are doing to rebuild your credit.

You also can contact the creditor and try to persuade them to take the negative information off of your report. Of course, this will depend on how bad the problem is or how often you may have been late on your payments, but it's always worth trying. A creditor can legally remove anything it has reported whenever it wants to.

Adding Accounts To Your Credit File

When you review your credit report, you may discover that it does not reflect all of your credit accounts. Although most major credit accounts will be included in your file, not all creditors supply information to CRAs. Some travel, entertainment, gasoline card companies, local retailers, and credit unions are among the creditors that don't provide such information.

If you've been told that you were denied credit because of an "insufficient credit file" or "no credit file" and you know you have accounts with creditors that don't appear in your credit file, ask the CRA to add this information to future reports. Although they are not required to do so, most CRAs will add verifiable accounts for a fee. However, you should understand that if these creditors do not report to the CRAs regularly, the added items will not be updated in your credit report.

To request that a CRA add accounts to you credit report, you should send them a Letter Requesting Inclusion Of Additional Accounts (see Chapter 8 "Letters") along with verification of the accounts, such as copies of recent statements. You also may contact the creditor(s) directly and ask that they report the information to the CRAs.

Other Options To Resolve A Credit Dispute

If you can't get any satisfaction from a CRA or a creditor and believe that you aren't being treated fairly, you can contact the agencies to which they report and/or file a formal complaint with the Federal Trade Commission (FTC).

Creditor Regulatory Agencies

If you have questions about your credit rights or feel a creditor has treated you unfairly, you may consider contacting the appropriate regulatory agency listed below.

Creditor	Contact
National Banks	Office of the Comptroller of the Currency Customer Assistance Unit 1301 McKinney St. Suite 3710 Houston, TX 77010 (800)613-6743; http://www.occ.treas.gov
	Federal Credit Unions National Credit Union Association Office of Public And Congressional Affairs 1775 Duke Street Alexandria, VA 22314 (703) 518-6330; http://www.ncua.gov
Savings and Loan Associations	Office of Thrift Supervision Consumer Programs 17010 G Street, N.W., 6th Floor Washington, DC 20552 (800)842-6929; http://www.ots.treas.gov.
Savings and Loan	Office of Thrift Supervision Office of Consumer Affairs 1700 G Street, N.W. Washington, D.C. 20552
Credit Union	National Credit Union Association Division of Consumer Affairs

1776 g Street, N.W.
Washington, D.C. 20456

Other creditors, such as department stores,

Finance companies, etc.

Federal Trade Commission
Division of Credit Practices
Pennsylvania Avenue at Sixth
Street, N.W.
Washington, D.C. 20580

If you have an unsatisfied complaint against a CRA, you might also consider filing a formal complaint against the company with the FTC. The FTC works for the consumer to prevent fraudulent, deceptive and unfair business practices in the marketplace. It enters Internet, telemarketing, identity theft and other fraud-related complaints into Consumer Sentinel, a secure, online database available to hundreds of civil and criminal law enforcement agencies in the U.S. and abroad. The more complaints filed against a company, such as a CRA, the more likely the FTC is to take action against the company.

In your letter of complaint to the FTC, you should explain your credit record problem(s) and provide a detailed account of everything you have done to try and resolve the matter and the negative results you have received. Include copies of any letters, notices or other documentation you may have to back up you complaint. See chapter 8 in this book for an example of a formal complaint letter you may send to the Federal Trade Commission.

Even though the FTC can't act as your lawyer in private credit disputes, information about your experiences and concerns is vital to the enforcement of the FCRA and protecting your rights under the law. Send your questions or complaints to:

Consumer Response Center - FCRA
Federal Trade Commission
Washington, DC 20580.

You also can file a formal complaint online at the FTC's web site:

http://www.ftc.gov, or by calling toll-free, 1-877-FTC-HELP (1-877-382-4357).

Exercising Your Legal Rights

Among the rights granted to consumers is the right to sue a CRA, a user or — in some cases — a provider of CRA data, in state or federal court for most violations of the FCRA. If you win such a lawsuit, the defendant will have to pay damages and reimburse you for attorney fees to the extent ordered by the court.

Since some states have their own credit reporting laws, you should contact your state's office of consumer affairs or your state's Attorney General's office to find out whether or not your state has such laws and to find out if you should use your state's laws instead of the FCRA as the grounds for your lawsuit. It's also a good idea to consult an attorney who has had some experience filing FCRA-related lawsuits

If you do bring a lawsuit against a CRA or a creditor, here are the penalties they must pay if you win:

* **Fair Credit Reporting Act.** You may sue any credit-reporting agency or creditor for breaking the rules about who may see your credit records or for not correcting errors in your file. You are entitled to actual damages, plus punitive damages that the court may allow if the violation is proved to have been intentional. If you win, you also will be awarded court costs and attorney's fees. A person who obtains a credit report without proper authorization or an employee of a CRA who gives a credit report to unauthorized persons may be fined up to $5,000 or sent to prison for one year, or both.

* **Truth in Lending and Consumer Leasing Acts**. If any creditor fails to disclose information required under these Acts, or gives inaccurate information, or does not comply with the rules about credit cards or the right to cancel home-secured loans, you as an individual may sue for actual damages and any money loss you suffer. In addition, you can sue for twice the finance charge in the case of certain disclosures, or, if a lease is concerned, 25 percent of the total monthly payments. In both cases, the least the court may award you if you win is 4100, and the most is $1,000. In any lawsuit that you win, you also are entitled to reimbursement for court costs and attorney's fees.

* **Equal Credit Opportunity Act**. If you believe that you can prove that a cred-

itor has discriminated against you for any reason prohibited by this act, you may sue for actual damages plus punitive damages — that is, damages for the fact that the law has been violated — of up to $10,000. If you win such a lawsuit, the court also will award you court costs and a reasonable amount for attorney's fees.

* **Fair Credit Billing Act.** Under this law, a creditor who breaks the rules for the correction of billing errors automatically loses the amount owed on the item in question and any finance charges on it, up to a combined total of $50, even if the bill was correct. As an individual, you also may sue for actual damages plus twice the amount of any finance charges, but in any case not less than $100 nor more than $1,000. You're also entitled to court costs and attorney's fees if your lawsuit is successful.

Opting Out

Creditors and insurers legally may use CRA file information as a basis for sending you unsolicited offers. You know, those pre-approved credit-card offers or the dinner-time telemarketing calls. These offers must include a toll-free number for you to call if you want to remove your name and address from lists (opt out) for two years. Completing a form that the CRA provides for this purpose will keep your name off such lists permanently

Here's how to opt out of the marketing lists of the big three CRAs:

* Equifax: To opt out of Equifax mailing lists, call 1-800-567-8688, or write to:

Equifax Credit Information Services
P.O. Box 740241
Atlanta, GA 30374

Include your complete name and current address with your request.

* Experian: You can contact this CRA directly to be removed from its marketing lists by calling toll-free 1-800-407-1088, or by sending your complete name (including any name variations you may use), mailing address and telephone number to:
Experian Consumer Services
901 West Bond Street

Lincoln, NE 68521

You should specify if you want to be removed from Experian's mailing lists or telemarketing lists, or both.

* TransUnion: If you want you name and address removed from mailing lists obtained from TransUnion, call 1-888-50OPTOUT (888-567-8688), or write to the following address:

TransUnion LLC's Name Removal Option
P.O. Box 97328
Jackson, MS 39288-7328

Include the following information with your request:

> First, middle, and last names (including Jr. Sr., III)
> Current address
> Previous address (if you've moved with the last six months)
> Date of birth
> Signature

Chapter 4

How To Deal With Debt

A sudden, unexpected illness or loss of your job may make it impossible for you to pay your bills on time. Whatever your situation, if you find that you can't pay your bills on time, you're not alone. Many people are faced with severe financial difficulties at sometime in their lives. Whether the situation is caused by personal or family illness, the loss of a job, or simple money mismanagement, mounting debt can seem overwhelming. The good news is, your financial situation doesn't have to go from bad to worse.

The fact is there are several debt management options available that can help you reduce your present debt and successfully rebuild your credit. In this chapter, we'll look at several of those options, including debt assessment and budgeting, negotiating with your creditors, credit counseling from a creditable organization, debt consolidation, and, as a last resort, bankruptcy. Which option works best for you depends on your level of debt, your level of discipline, and, of course, your prospects for the future.

Debt Assessment

The first step toward taking control of your financial situation is to do a "realistic' assessment of how much money you have coming in and how much you spend. Start by listing your income from all sources. Then, list your "fixed" expenditures - those bills that are the same each month - such as mortgage payments, rent, car payments, and insurance premiums. Next, list the expenses that vary, such as clothing, entertainment or recreation. Recording all your expenses — even those that may seem insignificant - is a helpful way to keep track of your spending patterns. It also helps you identify expenses that are necessary, and prioritize the rest. Your goal should be to make ends meet on the basics: housing, food, health care, insurance, and education.

Establishing A Budget

The debt assessment worksheet below will show you how much money you have coming in and how much you're spending. Fill in the monthly dollar amounts for each item in the worksheet, then subtract your total expenditures from your total income.

The result is the amount you can save without making any changes in your spending habits. Most financial consultants recommend a savings rate of 10% of your take-home pay. If you discover that your total is a negative number or less than you would like to save, you should make an attempt to find areas where you can cut spending. You can begin by keeping track of all your expenditures for one month (cash, check and credit). Look for areas where you can cut back. Maybe you can rent videos rather than going to the movies every weekend, use coupons at the grocery store, car pool to work or take your lunch rather than eating out.

One you've determined just how much you can save each month enter that amount on the worksheet as one of your permanent expenditures. The idea is to pay yourself first by setting aside your savings as soon as you receive your paycheck, before you're tempted to spend the money on something else. It also helps to have savings deducted automatically from your paycheck or checking account.

Sample Budget Worksheet

Income		Expenditures	
Your Salary	________	Rent/Mortgage	________
Spouse's Salary	________	Utilities (phone, cable, gas, electric)	________
Bonuses	________	Insurance (home/health/ life/auto)	________
Commissions	________	Food	________
Tips	________	Clothing	________
Interest Income	________	Debt Obligations (alimony/child support/credit card balances)	________
Rental Income	________	Child Care	________
Social Security Income	________	Medical/ DentalExpenses	________
Pension Income	________	Taxes	________
		Alimony	________
		Transportation (car payments, gas, tolls)	________
Other	________	Personal	

(toiletries/allowances) ________________

Gifts
(birthdays/ showers/charities)

- - - - - - - - - - - - - - - - -

Recreation/Movies ________________

____

Other ________________

Total Income ________________ **Total Expenditures** ________________

Subtract Total Expenditures from Total Income ________________

You can get more free information about budgeting and money managing techniques at your public library. Low cost budget counseling services that can help you analyze your income and expenses and develop a budget and spending plan also are available in most communities (see below). Look in your local Yellow Pages or contact your local bank or consumer protection office for information about these services.

Contacting Your Creditors

Many people make the mistake of hoping that creditors will simply give up and forget a debt that isn't repaid. Simply put, creditors don't forget. If you owe them money, they expect to be paid. And obviously, you should make good any obligations you have taken on to best of your ability. However, if you are having trouble making ends meet, you shouldn't hide or ignore the problem, you should instead "take the bull by the horns" and contact your creditors immediately.

When you contact the creditor, explain why it is difficult for you to meet the obligation, and request a modified payment plan that reduces your payments to a more manageable level. Whatever you do, don't wait until your accounts have been turned over to a debt collector. At that point, the creditors have given up on you and have likely turned your account over to a collection agency.

The fact is, most creditors don't want to spend their time and money trying to collect delinquent accounts — they just want their money. That's why, in most cases, creditors are willing to work with debtors through their financial crisis. For example, you may want to offer your creditor interest payments on your principal until your financial condition changes. In addition, you should check to see whether or not your debt is covered by a payment protection plan or some other insurance plan that would pay your debt. In some cases creditors may be willing to accept partial payment as satisfaction in full for the amount that you owe. But none of this will happen unless you take the initiative and open an honest and continuing dialogue with your creditors.

Requesting A Debt Repayment Plan

Before you contact a creditor to request a repayment plan on an overdue account, you'll need to determine just how much you can afford to pay. Don't over- or under-estimate the amount. And regardless of the creditor's initial response, don't give in and agree to pay more than you can realistically afford. Otherwise, you'll remain in the same no-win financial situation — in debt, and unable to pay off the account.

The key to success in getting a workable debt repayment plan is persistence. It may take several calls and/or letters (see Chapter 8 "Letters" to get the creditor to agree to a reduced payment you both can live with. Just remember, to a creditor, some money is better than no money at all, so most are willing to make a workable agreement.

In your initial contact with a creditor regarding your overdue account, you should be polite, but firm. Explain clearly that you're having difficulty making your payments and why, and that you want to make a payment arrangement that you can afford. Make sure the creditor understands that the amount of payment you suggest is all that you can afford, and that you do intend to make payment in full eventually, even if you know that may not be possible.

Obviously, before a creditor agrees to any new payment plan, they will want to know why you're having problems meeting the original agreement. The best policy here is honesty. Tell them truthfully why you're having trouble - perhaps it's because you recently lost your job, have unexpected medical bills, or have just gone through a divorce. Most creditors are willing to work with you and will appreciate your honesty and forthrightness.

Finally, if you are able to work out a satisfactory debt repayment plan, ask your creditor (s) to report your new, reduced payments to the CRA as being on time. Otherwise, the CRA may continue to report these payments as "past due" because you're paying less than the amount agreed to in your original credit agreement.

In the unlikely event that that you cannot come to an agreement on a debt repayment plan, and you can not pay off what you owe in a timely manner, you then may be forced to deal with collection agencies, or debt collectors. If that's the case, you should know what to expect and what rights you have as provided by law.

Dealing With Debt Collectors

Here are the cold hard facts: if you use credit cards, owe money on a personal loan, or are paying for a home mortgage, you are a "debtor". Furthermore, if you fall behind in repaying your creditors, or an error is made on your accounts, you may be contacted by a "debt collector".

Admittedly that all sound sounds rather scary — and if you are indeed a debtor it can be —but the good news is, as a consumer, you have the law on your side. In this case, it's the Fair Debt Collection Act (FDCA). The Fair Debt Collections Act requires that debt collectors treat you fairly by prohibiting certain methods of debt collection. Obviously, however, the law does not forgive any legitimate debt you may owe.

So, what happens when the collection agency keeps calling you at the office and bothering you at home, sometimes calling as late as 11 p.m.? Can you legally do anything besides fume and hang up the phone? The FDCA says you can, if you have personal, family and household debts, including money owed for the purchase of an automobile, for medical care, or for charge accounts.

Your Rights Under The Fair Debt Collection Act

The FDCA is the federal law that dictates how and when a debt collector may contact you. Basically, the law prohibits debt collectors from calling you at home before 8 a.m., or after 9 p.m., or at work if the collector knows that your employer doesn't approve of the calls. Collectors may not harass you, make false statements, or use unfair practices when they try to collect a debt. Debt collectors also must honor a written request from you to stop further contact.

Here is a further summary of your rights under the FDCA:

* You can stop a debt collector from contacting you by writing a letter to the collection agency telling them to cease all communications with you (see chapter 8 "Letters"). Once they agency receives your letter, it may not contact you again, except to inform you that there will be no further contact or to notify you that the debt collector or creditor intends to take some specific action. You can send such a letter, even if the collector is not breaking the law. Understand, however, that sending such a letter to a collector does not release you from any debts you actually owe. You could still be sued by the debt collector or by your original creditor.

* A debt collector may not contact any third parties, other than your attorney about your debt. If you don't have an attorney, a collector may contact other people - a CRA, the original creditor, etc. - but only to find out where you live, your phone number, and where you work. Collectors usually are not allowed to contact such third parties more than once, and in most cases may not tell anyone other than you and your attorney that you owe money.

* Within five days after you are first contacted about the debt, a collector must send you a written notice telling you the amount of money you owe, the name of the creditor to whom you owe the money; and what action to take if you believe you don't owe the money.

* A debt collector may not continue to contact you if, within 30 days after you receive the written notice, you send the collection agency a letter stating that you do not owe money. However, a collector can renew collection efforts if you are sent proof of the debt, such as a copy of a bill for the amount owed.

Types of Debt Collection Practices Prohibited by the FDCA

Harassment
It's illegal for a debt collector to harass, oppress, or abuse anyone or any third

parties they contact. For example, debt collectors may not:

* use threats of violence or harm;
* publish a list of consumers who refuse to pay their debts (except to a credit bureau);
* use obscene or profane language; or
* repeatedly use the telephone to annoy someone;

False Statements

It's against the law for debt collectors to use any false statements when collecting s debt. For example, debt collectors may not:

* falsely claim that they are attorneys or government representatives;
* claim that you have committed a crime;
* falsely represent that the operate or work for a credit bureau;
* claim that you owe more than you do;
* indicate that papers being sent to you are legal forms when they are not; or
* indicate that papers being sent to you are not legal forms when they are.

In addition, debt collectors also may not state that:

* you will be arrested if you don't pay your debt;
* they will seize, garnish, attach, or sell your property or wages, unless the collection agency or creditor actually intends to do so; or
* actions, such as a lawsuit, will be taken against you, which legally may not be taken, or which they don't really intend to take.

The FDCA also says that debt collectors may not:

* give false credit information about you to anyone, including a credit vureau;
* send you anything that looks like an official document from a court or government agency when it is not; or
* use a false name

Unfair Practices

It's illegal for debt collectors to engage in unfair practices when they try to collect a debt. Under the law, debt collectors may not:

* collect any amount greater than your debt, unless your state law permits such a charge:
* deposit a post-dated check prematurely;
* use deception to make you accept collect calls or pay for telegrams;
* take or threaten to take your property unless it can be done legally; or
* contact you by postcard.

What You Can Do If you Believe a Debt Collector Has Violated the FDCA

First of all you should understand that if you owe more than one debt, any payment you make must be applied to the debt you indicate. It's against the law for a debt collector to apply any payment you make to any debt you believe you do not owe. If you believe that a debt collector has violated this or any other right you have under the FDCA, you have four options:

1) Tell The Collector to "Cease and Desist." Under the FDCA you have the right to tell a collection agency to stop contacting you. And that's simply a matter of sending a letter stating that you want the collection agency to immediately cease all communications with you.

2) Document all suspected illegal behavior. If a debt collector violates the FDCA, you should document the violation immediately. Maintain a written record of what happened, when it happened and who witnesses it. Then, try to have another person present (or on the phone) during all future conversations with the collector. Some states allow you to record phone conversations without the collector's knowledge. In others, recording phone conversations is illegal. Your state consumer protection agency can tell you whether you can record such phone conversations in your state.

3) File a formal complaint. You can file an official complaint with the Federal Trade Commission (FTC), the federal agency that oversees collection agencies. Ask the FTC to send you a complaint form, or just write a letter (see sample letter to FTC in Chapter 8). You can contact the Federal Trade Commission at 6th and Pennsylvania Ave. NW, Washington, DC 20580; http://www.ftc.gov/ftc/complaint.htm. Be sure to include the collection agency's name and address, the name of the collector, the dates and times of the conversations, and the names of any witnesses. In addition, you should attach copies of any offending materials you received and a copy of any tape you made.

You also should send a copy of your complaint to the state agency that regulates collection agencies for the state where the agency is located. You can find the agency by calling information in the state's capitol. In addition, send a copy to the original creditor and the collection agency. This may cause the original creditor some concern about its own liability in the matter and could lead to it canceling the debt.

4) Sue the debt collector.

Under the FDCA, you have the right to sue a debt collector in a state or federal court within one year from the date the law was violated. If you win, you may recover money for the damages you suffered plus an additional amount up to $1,000. Court costs and attorney fees also can be recovered. A group of people also may sue a debt collector and recover money for damages up to $500,000, or one percent of the collector's net worth, whichever is less.

While the law is on your side, it does frown on frivolous suits. Before you take that step, make sure you have been the victim of repeated abusive behavior, clearly in violation of the FDCA. If the "illegal behavior" never goes beyond just being annoying, you should not consider a law suit.

By law, you can represent yourself in small claims court, or you can hire an attorney and take the case to regular court. As already noted, the collector may have to pay your attorney's fees and court costs if you win.

Credit Counseling

If you find that you aren't disciplined enough to create, and stick-to a workable budget, can't work out a repayment plan with your creditors, or simply can't deal with your mounting debt, you may want to consider contacting a credit counseling service. Most creditors are willing to accept reduced payments if you enter into a debt repayment plan with a reputable company.

Through a debt repayment plan, you deposit money each month with the credit counseling service. Your deposits are used to pay your creditors according to a payment schedule developed by the counselor. As part of the repayment plan, you may have to agree not to apply for, or use any additional credit as long as you are participating in the program.

A successful repayment plan requires you to make regular, timely payments, and could take 4 years or longer to complete. You should ask the credit counseling service you are considering using for an estimate of the time it will take you to complete the plan. Some credit counseling services charge little or nothing at all for managing your debt repayment plan. Others charge a monthly fee that could result in a significant amount of money over time.

While it's true that a debt repayment plan can eliminate much of the stress that comes from dealing with overdue bills and creditors, it doesn't mean you can just forget about your debts. Quite the contrary — you are still responsible for paying any creditors whose debts are not included in the plan. You also are responsible for reviewing monthly statements from your creditors to make sure your payments have been received. And in some cases a repayment plan depends on creditors agreeing to lower or eliminate interest and finance charges, or waive late fees. If you sign up for such a plan, you will be responsible for making sure these concessions are shown on your statements.

You should also know that a credit counseling service doesn't erase your negative history. As you know, accurate information about your accounts can stay on your credit report for up to seven years. In addition, your creditors will continue to report information about your accounts that are handled through a debt repayment plan. For example, some creditors may report that an account is in financial counseling, that payments have been late or missed altogether, or that there are write-offs or other concessions. However, if you demonstrate a pattern of timely payments, you should be able to get credit in the future.

There are non-profit credit counseling organizations in every state that counsel consumers in debt. Counselors try to arrange repayment plans that are acceptable to you and your creditors. These services also can help you set up a realistic and workable budget. The best part is that these services are typically offered at little or no cost to consumers. You can find the nearest credit counseling office by checking the White Pages of your telephone directory.

In addition, some non-profit counseling programs are operated by universities, military bases, credit unions, and housing authorities. They also are likely to charge little or nothing for their services. You also can check with your local bank or consumer protection office to see if it has a list of reputable, low-cost credit counseling services available.

You also can contact Neighborhood Housing Services, which offers free financial counseling. It has offices in every major U.S. city. Refer to the organization's web site at: http://www.nw.org. The HUD website, http://www.HUD.gov lists approved counseling agencies that help homeowners in financial trouble.

Choosing The Right Credit Counselor

If you do decide to work with a credit counseling agency, you should make an effort to interview several potential services. Below are some questions to ask during those interviews:

Regarding Services And Fees

* What services do you offer?
* Do you have any educational materials? If so, will you send to me? Are they free? Are they available on the Internet?
* In addition to helping me solve my immediate money problems, will you also help me develop a plan for avoiding problems in the future?
* What are your fees? Do I have to pay anything upfront before you can help me? Are there monthly fees? What the basis for the fees?
* What is your source of funding?
* Will I have a formal written agreement or contract with you?
* How soon can you begin working with me?
* Who regulates, oversees and/or licenses your agency? Is your agency audited?
* Are your counselors accredited or certified? If not, how are they trained?
* Can you assure me that the information about me (including my address and phone number) will be kept confidential?

Regarding A Repayment Plan

* How deep in debt do I have to be to use your services?
* How do you decide on the amount of my payment? What happens if you want more than I can afford to pay?
* How does your debt repayment plan work?
* How will I know my creditors have received payments?
* How often will I get status reports on my accounts?

* Will I have access to my accounts online or by phone?
* Can you get my creditors to lower or waive interest and finance charges or waive late fees?
* Is a debt repayment plan my only option?
* What debts will be excluded from the debt repayment plan?
* Will you help me plan for payment of these debts, as well?
* Who will help me if I have problems with my accounts or creditors?
* Is the information I provide to you secure?

How To Deal With Your Auto And Home Loans

While debt repayment plans typically cover unsecured debt, your auto and home loan, which are considered secured debt, may not be included. There's no way around it (unless you want to lose your vehicle or your home), you must continue to make payments to these accounts directly.

Most automobile financing arrangements allow a creditor to repossess your car any time you're in default. That's not exactly a position you want to be in. If your vehicle is repossessed, you may have to pay the full balance due on the loan. And to add insult to injury, you also might have to pay towing and storage costs, as well, to get it back. If you aren't financially able to do that, the creditor may sell the car. If you see such a situation arising, you may be better off selling the car yourself and paying off the debt. That way, you would avoid the added costs of repossession and the addition of a negative entry on your credit report.

Should you fall behind on your mortgage, contact your lender immediately to avoid foreclosure. Contrary to popular belief, most lenders are not hard-hearted penny pinchers, just waiting to take you property from you. In fact, most lenders are willing to work with you if they believe that you're acting in good faith and that your financial situation is only temporary. Some lenders may even reduce or suspend your payments for a short time. When you resume regular payments, though, you may have to pay an additional amount toward the past due amount. Other lenders may agree to change the terms of the mortgage by extending the repayment period to reduce the monthly debt. You should find out whether or not the additional fees would be assessed for these changes, and calculate how much they add up to over the long run.

If you and the lender can't work out a payment plan, contact a housing counseling agency. Some agencies limit their counseling service to homeowners with FHA mortgages, but many offer free help to homeowners who are having trouble making their mortgage payments. Contact your local office of the Department of Housing and Urban Development (HUD) or the housing authority in your state, city, or county for help in finding a housing counseling agency near you.

Debt Consolidation

Another option for lowering the cost of your monthly debt is consolidating your debt through a home equity line of credit, or a personal loan. In either case, the loan allows you to combine all of your monthly bills into one fixed monthly payment — up to 50% lower than what you may currently be paying. The difference between these two types of debt consolidation loans is that a home equity loan allows you to borrow against the value of your home (collateral), whereas a personal debt consolidation loan is usually not backed by a home or any other collateral but rather relies on your "promise" to repay.

Home Equity Loan

Statistics compiled over the past five years show that more and more homeowners are using home equity loans to pay off credit-card and other debt. According to the Federal Reserve, American homeowners borrowed a total of $701.5 billion from their home equity in 2002, up from $416.2 billion just five years ago. Low home equity rates and, increasingly high credit-card rates, have apparently convinced millions of homeowners that this type of debt consolidation loan is the best option.

The thing to think about long and hard before using this option is that these loans require your home as collateral. If you can't make the payments, or if the payments are late, you could lose your home. You also should understand that the cost of these consolidation loans can add up. In addition to interest on the loan, you'll be required to pay "points." Typically, one point is equal to one percent of the amount you borrow. Still, these loans may provide certain tax advantages that aren't available with other kinds of credit, such as a personal loan. For example, the interest paid on a home equity loan is usually tax deductible.

Personal Loan

Using a personal loan to consolidate your debt can help. As with a home equity loan, instead of paying multiple bills, you can pay just one, perhaps with lower monthly payments. However, before taking this option, there are a few things to consider, as well.

First of all, personal loans typically come with interest rates of 14% to 15% — and that's for people with good credit! If your reason for considering such a loan is trouble dealing with heavy debts or bad credit, you'll likely end up paying anywhere from 18% to 21% or higher. You also may have to cough up upfront fees of as much as 10% of the loan amount.

Of course, if you can secure a low-rate, low-cost loan and pay off your debt faster than you might be able to otherwise, then this type of debt consolidation loan might be your best option.

The bottom line when considering debt consolidation as a solution to dealing with debt is, first of all it usually does little if anything at all to solve the problem that got the debtor in trouble in the first place. These loans also can be far more expensive than the debt they're designed to pay off, and can contain hidden fees, expensive insurance, and other money-makers for lenders.

Personal Bankruptcy

The last option for dealing with debt that we will consider in this chapter is personal bankruptcy. We've "saved" this option for last because it generally is considered the debt management tool of last resort, because the results are long-lasting and far-reaching. As explained in previous chapters, a bankruptcy stays on your credit report for 10 years, making it difficult to acquire new credit, buy a home, get life insurance, or sometimes a job. However, it is a legal procedure which can give people who cannot pay their bills a fresh start. Individuals who follow the bankruptcy rules receive a discharge, which is a court order that says they do not have to repay certain debts.

There are two main types of bankruptcy available to individuals: Chapter 7 and Chapter 13. Each must be filed in federal bankruptcy court. In Chapter 7, your nonexempt assets may be sold to pay creditors while most of your debts are discharged. In Chapter 13, you prepare a reorganization plan to pay off creditors in full or in part. Once you file a bankruptcy petition, an automatic stay prevents creditors from starting or continuing most legal proceedings against you.

Repaying Debts Through Chapter 7 Bankruptcy

Chapter 7, also knows as "straight bankruptcy", involves liquidating all your assets that are not exempt. Exempt property may include cars, work-related tools and basic household furnishings. Some of your property may be sold by a court-appointed trustee, or turned over to creditors. In most cases however, you may not have to give up any of your personal property. Typically you can choose either the exemptions provided in the Bankruptcy Code or those allowed under your state law, whichever is most beneficial. Creditors do retain the right to any collateral you have pledged to secure a loan

The first step in Chapter 11 is to file a petition and required schedules at the clerk's office of the federal bankruptcy court. Your petition must include a list of all your creditors, the sources of your income, a list of all your real and personal property, and a complete list detailing all of your living expenses. Here are the main documents you'll need:

* Deeds, mortgages, contracts on your home and mortgage statements.

* Copies of tax returns for the past two years.

* All legal papers, summonses, complaints and notices of attachment, execution or garnishment.

* Credit card bills, medical bills and any other documents regarding outstanding debt.

* Statements and passbooks for savings and checking accounts for the past year.

* Student loan papers.

You can get the required forms from the court clerk. To find the number of the local bankruptcy court, check the federal government listings in the white pages of your phone directory. The current fees for seeking bankruptcy relief are about $175, and are payable at the time you file your petition. Under some circumstances, the court may allow you to pay the fee in installments. And a few courts waive the fee altogether for individuals who are indigent.

Unless your filing is very basic, it's advisable to hire an attorney, which of course, is another expense. Attorney fees may range from $400 to $1,000 or more, depending on the complexity of your case. Just be sure to discuss attorney fees at the outset, and find out whether or not you can pay the fee in installments.

In a Chapter 7 filing, the entire procedure typically takes from four to six months. And, you can file for Chapter 7 bankruptcy only once every six years, and again, the notice of filing usually will stay on your credit report for up to 10 years. You also should understand that although your debt may be discharged, anyone who has co-signed a loan with you is still responsible, even after your bankruptcy.

Chapter 13 Bankruptcy

If you have a regular income, Chapter 13 bankruptcy allows you to keep property, such as a mortgaged house or car, that you otherwise might lose. It provides a method for repaying your debt over a period of time — generally from three to five years - according to a court-approved plan. In most cases, only an individual with unsecured debts of less than $270,000 and secured debts of less than $800,000 is eligible to file for this type of bankruptcy.

To file Chapter 13, you need to file the appropriate schedules and petitions with the federal bankruptcy court and pay the filing fee. You also are required to file a proposed plan of repayment with your original petition or within the next 15 days. A court-appointed trustee will supervise your performance, to make regular payments to your creditors and to provide the court and other involved parties with information about your debts.

Nondischargeable Debts

While both types of bankruptcy may get rid of unsecured debts and stop foreclosures, repossessions, garnishments, utility shut-offs, and debt collection activities there are some debts that can't be discharged through either Chapter 7 or Chapter 13. These include certain, taxes, alimony and child support, student loans and some property settlements. Other debts that cannot be discharged through bankruptcy result from fraud, willful or malicious injury, certain fines or penalties, and claims incurred from driving under the influence of alcohol or drugs.

As you know, a bankruptcy filing generally will remain on your credit record for up to ten years, but it doesn't have to be a permanent credit handicap. That's because there are laws that forbid discrimination against individuals who have declared bankruptcy. For example, you may not be denied or evicted from public housing or be denied a driver's license just because you filed for bankruptcy.

A Fresh Start Through Bankruptcy

There's no doubt that bankruptcy does severe damage to your credit report. But, it still is possible to regain confidence among creditors. You usually can obtain more credit if you demonstrate a consistent and signs that your financial situation is improving. You can start rebuilding your credit by opening a savings account and obtaining a secured credit card. Make all payments on time to build a positive credit file.

During your credit rebuilding period, you should check your credit report regularly to make sure you are getting credit for your efforts. Refer to Chapter 2, for information on how to obtain a copy of your credit report.

And finally, before you make the critical decision to file for personal bankruptcy, you might consider contacting a credit counselor or consult with an attorney and try to reach out-of-court agreements with your creditors. While bankruptcy is a legal option for debt repayment, it generally should be your option of last resort.

Chapter 5

How To Avoid Credit-Related Scams

With consumer debt at an all-time high, and a record number of consumers filing for bankruptcy, it's small wonder why con artists are crawling out of the woodwork with credit-related schemes and scams. Unfortunately, many people, burdened by mounting debt, turn to these crooks, who, in the guise of legitimate businesses, promise help in solving debt problems.

Whether a debt dilemma is the result of an illness, unemployment, or overspending it can seem overwhelming. It also can create a serious vulnerability sought by con artists looking for "easy prey". That's where many credit repair companies enter the picture.

Credit Repair Company Scams

Every day companies nationwide appeal to consumers with poor credit records. You see these appeals in ads in newspapers, on TV and on the Internet. You may even get calls from telemarketers offering credit repair services. They all make the same claims. They all promise, for a fee ranging from $50 to $2,000 or more, to "clean-up" your credit report so you can get a car loan, a home mortgage, insurance, or even a job.

Some of these credit repair companies are legitimate businesses that operate within the law to help consumers resolve various credit-related problems and rebuild their credit. They typically provide their "services" for a substantial fee. Many of these companies, however, are bogus, claiming to erase bad credit completely, or that they can help consumers "create a new credit identity", or even remove bankruptcies, judgments, liens, and bad loans for consumer credit records forever. The problem with these companies is that that can't deliver on their outlandish claims. After you pay them hundreds or thousands of dollars, these companies do nothing to improve your credit report; most simply take your money and run.

Before responding to a credit repair company offer, you should understand that these companies cannot do anything for you that you can't do yourself for little or no cost at all. As explained in preceding chapters, the FCRA gives you the right to have inaccurate or outdated information removed from your credit report and to have written statements attached to your credit report. The only costs you may incur are up to $9 for a copy of your credit report and postage.

You also should keep in mind that negative accurate information can not be removed from your credit report until the law says it can - from 7 to 10 years. Neither you nor a credit repair company can change the law to alter your credit report in your favor. The thing to remember when dealing with these companies is that the FCRA is on your side - credit repair companies are just out to get your money, usually any way they can - legally or not.
How To Recognize The Warning Signs Of A Credit Repair Scam

If you do decide to respond to a credit repair company offer, you should be suspicious of companies that:

* ask you to pay for credit repair services before any services are provided;

* don't tell you your legal rights and what you can do yourself for free;

* claim they get you a major credit card despite your credit history;

* recommend that you not contact a credit bureau directly;

* suggest that you try to invent a "new" credit report by applying for an Employer Identification Number to use instead of your Social Security number; or

* advise you to dispute all the information in your credit report or take action that seems illegal, such as creating a new identity. If you do follow illegal advice and commit fraud, you may be subject to prosecution.

You could be charged and prosecuted for mail or wire fraud if you use the mail or telephone to apply for credit and provide false information. It's a federal crime to make false statements on a loan or credit application, to misrepresent your Social Security number, and to obtain and Employer Identification number from the IRS under false pretenses. Don't let a credit repair company suggest otherwise.

Advance Fee Loan Scams

Most lenders are owned and operated by legitimate professionals. But fraudulent loan brokers and other individuals misrepresenting the availability of credit and credit terms definitely are in business. And one of their favorite strategies is the "advance fee" loan. That's a scam that typically targets consumers with credit problems or consumers who have difficulty getting credit. In exchange for an up-front fee, these companies guarantee that applicants will get the credit they want - usually a credit card or a personal loan.

Some companies claim that they can guarantee you a loan for a fee paid in advance. The fee may range from $100 to several hundred dollars. In some cases, small businesses have been charged as much as several thousand dollars as an advance fee for a loan. It makes no difference if you're an individual consumer or an owner of a small business - the scam works the same — you don't get the money you wanted, the con artist does. And once they have your money, they vanish.

You should resist the temptation to "cash-in" on advance-fee loan guarantees. They may, in fact, be illegal. Most legitimate creditors offer extensions of credit, such as credit cards, loans, and mortgages, through telemarketing and require an application fee or
appraisal fee in advance. However, legitimate creditors never guarantee in advance that you'll get the loan. Under the federal Telemarketing Sales Rule, a seller or telemarketer who guarantees or represents a high likelihood of your getting a loan or some other extension of credit may not ask for or receive payment until you've received the loan.

How To Recognize An Advance-Fee Loan Scam

Unfortunately there are many fraudulent loan brokers and other individuals misrepresenting the availability of credit and credit terms. These companies claim to guarantee that they can get a loan or other type of credit for you - but you must pay a fee before you apply.

Ads that promise advance-fee loans typically appear in the classified section of local and national newspapers and magazines, and on the Internet. They also may appear in radio ads, on local cable stations, and in flyers circulated in neighborhoods and parking lots. Many of these "offers" feature "900" numbers, which result in charges on your phone bill, or toll-free "800" numbers. In addition, these companies often use delivery systems other than the U.S Postal Service, including overnight or courier services, in order to avoid detection and prosecution by postal authorities.

If you're considering such an offer, be sure you don't confuse a legitimate credit offer with an advance-fee loan scam. An offer for credit from a bank, mortgage broker, savings and loan, or credit union generally requires your verbal or written acceptance of the loan or credit offer. The offer typically is subject to a check of your credit report after you apply to make sure you meet their credit requirements. You usually are not required to pay a fee in order to get the credit.

The best advice is to be wary of anyone who contacts you by phone and tells you that he/she can guarantee that you will get a loan (or other credit) if you pay in advance. Just say no, and hang up the phone. The offer is against the law.

Protecting Yourself

Under the Telemarketing Sales Rule, if anyone guarantees or suggests that there is a "strong chance" that they can arrange a loan or other form of credit for you, and they ask you to pay a fee in advance, it's a scam. That's because it's against the law for anyone to ask you to pay, or to accept payment for their services before you get your promised loan or credit.

Here are some important facts to keep in mind when you are considering responding to an ad that promises "easy credit", regardless of your credit history:

* Most legitimate creditors will not "guarantee' that you will get a loan or a credit card before you apply, especially if you have a poor credit history, or a bankruptcy on your credit report.
* It is an accepted and common practice for reputable creditors to require payment for a credit report or appraisal. You also may be required to pay a processing or application fee.

* You should never give your credit card account number, bank account information, or Social Security number over the telephone or the Internet unless you are familiar with the company and you know why the information is necessary.

* If you don't have the offer in hand or otherwise confirmed in writing, and you are asked to pay a fee, decline the offer. It's fraud and it against the law.

If you think you've been a victim of an advance-fee loan scam, you should contact your local consumer protection agency, state Attorney General (see Appendix D) or local Better Business Bureau (BBB) to report the fraudulent company.

Secured Credit Card Marketing Scams

You've most likely seen the ads:

ANYONE CAN QUALIFY FOR A MAJOR CREDIT CARD!

BAD CREDIT? NO CREDIT? NO PROBLEM!

CALL 900-123-4567 TODAY!

Even if you've been turned down before, you owe it to yourself and your family to make the call NOW and get the credit you deserve! A major credit card is just one call away!

Admittedly, ads like this may appeal to anyone with a poor credit history or no credit at all, but the old maxim, "if it sounds too good to be true, it probably is", applies to this scam. While secured credit cards can be an effective way to build or re-establish your credit history, some companies that market secured cards make deceptive advertising claims to entice likely victims to respond to their ads.

Secured vs. Unsecured Cards

You know that secured and unsecured credit cards can be used to pay for goods and services. The difference between the two is that a secured credit card requires that you open and maintain a savings account as security for your line of credit. — an unsecured card does not.

The amount of money required for a savings deposit for a secured credit card may vary from a few hundred to several thousand dollars. Your credit line is a percentage of your total deposit, usually 50 to 100 percent. Typically, a bank will pay interest on your deposit. In addition, you also may have to pay application and processing fees — sometimes as much as several hundred dollars. Before you apply, you should ask what the total fees are and whether or not they will be refunded if you're denied a card. Usually, a secured card will require an annual fee and have a higher interest rate than an unsecured card.

The problem, many companies use deceptive ads, such as the one above to lure potential victims into purchasing a secured card. The Federal Trade Commission (FTC) has taken action against such companies that deceptively advertise major credit cards through television, newspapers and postcards. The ads may offer either unsecured or secured cards, or not specify a card type, and generally lead you to believe that you can get a card simply by calling the number listed. In many cases, the number listed is not toll-free. A "900" number service, such as shown in the example ad above, for which you are billed just for making the call, will usually instruct you to give your name and address to in order to receive a credit application, or give you a list of banks offering secured cards. It also may instruct you to call another "900" number - at an additional charge - for more information.

What these deceptive ads often leave out is the following:

> The cost of the "900" call - which can range from $2 to $50;
> The required security deposit, application, and processing fees:
> Eligibility requirements, such as income or age:
> An annual fee or the fact that the secured card has a higher than average

interest rate on any balance.

How To Avoid The Secured Card Scam

While it may be tempting to respond to such ads, especially if you are trying to establish, or rebuild your credit, you're better off taking a couple of deep breaths then calmly consider the following signs that may indicate a scam is afoot:

* Offers of easy credit. Considering what you've learned in previous chapters of this book, you should know that no one can guarantee to get you credit. As explained earlier, before deciding whether or not to give you credit, legitimate credit providers examine your credit report.

* A call to a "900" number for a credit card. 900 numbers are not toll-free. You pay for calls with that prefix, and you many never receive a credit card of any type.

* Credit cards offered by "credit repair" companies or "credit clinics." As noted earlier in this chapter, these businesses also may "offer" to clean-up your credit history for a fee. However, as you have learned, you can correct genuine mistakes or outdated information yourself by contacting CRAs directly. You don't need a middleman. What's more, only time and good credit habits will completely restore your credit worthiness.

Getting A Secured Card The Right Way

If you do decide to get a secured card as a way to build or re-establish your credit record, you should make sure that the card issuer reports to a CRA. If the issuer doesn't report to a credit bureau, the card won't be of any help in building a credit history.

If you're interested in applying for a secured credit card, you can contact the BankCard Holders of America (BHA), which provides a lists of companies offering secured cards (You also received a list of such institutions in one of the free reports as part of the Instant Credit Repair Kit.). To get the BankCard list, send a check or money order for $4.00 to: "Secured Credit Card List", BHA Customer Service, 524 Branch Drive, Salem, VA 24153.

File Segregation Credit Repair Scam

Consumers who have filed for bankruptcy are likely targets of a credit repair scheme called "file segregation." In this scheme, you are promised a chance to "hide" negative credit information by establishing a new credit identity. Now that may sound like a perfect solution, especially if you think that you won't get any credit as long as the bankruptcy appears in your credit report. There's just one small problem with this solution - it's illegal. If you fall for credit repair pitch and use it, you could face a substantial fine or even a prison sentence.

Here's how the file segregation scam usually works:

If you're having credit problems and have filed for bankruptcy, you may receive a letter from a credit repair company warning you about you inability to get credit cards, personal loans, or any other types of credit for 10 years. However, for a fee, the company promises to help you hide your bankruptcy and establish a new credit identity to use when you apply for credit. These companies also make pitches in classified ads, on radio and TV, as well as on the Internet.

If you pay the fee and sign up for the service, you may be instructed to apply for an Employer Identification Number (EIN) from the IRS, Typically, EINs, which resemble Social Security numbers, are used by businesses to report financial information to the IRS and the Social Security Administration. .

After you receive your EIN, the credit repair company will tell you how to use it in place of your Social Security number when you apply for credit. The credit repair company also will tell you how to use a new mailing address and some credit references.

To convince you to establish a new credit identity, the credit repair company will likely make a variety of false claims, which may include the following:

* You will not be able to get credit for 10 years (the period of time bankruptcy information may stay on your credit report). The truth is that each creditor has its own criteria for granting credit. While one may reject you application because of a bankruptcy, another may grant you credit soon after you filed for bankruptcy. And, given a new reliable, consistent payment record, your chances of getting credit will probably increase as time passes, without the "help" of a credit repair company.

* The company or "file segregation" program is affiliated with the federal government. This claim makes the scheme sound almost like a federal "witness protection program", which legally provides new identities. In fact, the federal government does not support or work with any companies that offer such programs.

* The "file segregation" program is legal. The truth is that it is a federal crime to make any false statements on a loan or credit application. The credit repair company may advise you to do just that. It's a federal crime to misrepresent your Social Security number. It also is a federal crime to obtain an EIN from the IRS under false pretenses. In addition, file segregation likely world constitute civil fraud, as well, under many state laws.

File segregation and the other credit repair company scams described in this chapter prey on consumers who are knee deep in debt and are looking for a "quick-fix" for their problems. Unfortunately, the techniques advised by credit repair companies to affect such quick-fixes are usually illegal. The good news is that there is another federal law that provides consumers with certain protections and rights when dealing with credit repair companies.

The Credit Repair Organizations Act

In 1996 the Congress of the United States made the following findings:

* Consumers have a vital interest in establishing and maintaining their credit worthiness and credit standing in order to obtain and use credit. As a result, consumers who have experienced credit problems may seek assistance from credit repair organizations which offer to improve the credit standing of such consumers.

* Certain advertising and business practices of some companies engaged in the business of credit repair services have worked a financial hardship upon consumers, particularly those of limited economic means and who are inexperienced in credit matters.

So begins the Credit Repair Organization Act (CROA), enacted by the federal government to:

1) Ensure that prospective buyers of the services of the of the credit repair

organizations are provided with the information necessary to make an informed decision regarding the purchase of such services; and

2) To protect the public from unfair or deceptive advertising and business practices by credit repair organizations.

Under the CROA, credit repair companies must give you a copy of the 'Consumer Credit File Rights Under State and Federal Law" before you sign a contract. They also must give you a written contract that spells out your rights and obligations. To protect your rights, you should read these documents carefully before signing the contract.

The CROA also contains other consumer protections regarding credit repair companies, including the following:

* A credit repair company can not make false claims about its services.

* A credit repair company can not charge you until it has completed the promised services.

* Credit repair companies can not perform any services until they have your signature on a written contract and have completed a three-day waiting period. During this time, you can cancel the contract without paying any fees.

* A credit repair company must provide consumers with a written contract explaining the services to be performed; the payment for those services, including the total cost; how long it will take to achieve the promised results; any guarantees they offer; and the company's name and business address.

* The "Consumer Credit File Rights Under State and Federal Law" disclosure statement must be worded exactly as the provisions spelled out in the CROA (see the full text of this disclosure state at the end of this chapter). It must inform you of your right to dispute inaccurate or out-of-date credit record information without the "assistance" of a credit repair company, as well as the right to obtain a copy of their credit report from a CRA. The disclosure statement also must provide an overview of consumer rights when working

with a credit repair company, including the right to sue the company if it violates the CROA.

* A credit repair company may not encourage consumers to change their identities in order to provide them with new, problem-free credit histories.

What To Do If You Are A Victim of A Credit-Related Scam

Under the law, you have the right to sue credit repair companies that violate the CROA. The law allows you to seek, in federal court, either your actual losses or the amount you paid the company - whichever is more. You also can seek "punitive" damages - sums of money to punish the company for violating the law. The Law also allows class actions in federal court - cases where groups of consumers join together in one lawsuit. If you win, the other side has to pay your attorney fees.
Many states also have laws regulating credit repair companies (see list below), and may be helpful if you've lost money to credit repair scams.

If you've had a problem with a credit repair company, don't be embarrassed or afraid to report it. Contact your local consumer affairs office or your state attorney general (see Appendix D). Many state attorney Generals have toll-free consumer hotlines

You also may consider filing a complaint with the Federal Trade Commission. As noted earlier, while the FTC cannot resolve individual credit problems for consumers, it can take action against a company if it receives enough complaints to establish a pattern of possible law violations. You can contact the FTC about a problem with a credit repair company by writing to: Consumer Response Center, Federal Trade Commission, Washington, D.C. 20580.

States With Laws Regulating Credit Repair Companies

* Arkansas
* Arizona
* California
* Colorado
* Connecticut
* Maryland
* Massachusetts
* Michigan
* Minnesota
* Missouri
* Texas
* Utah
* Virginia
* Washington
* West Virginia

* Delaware
* Florida
* Georgia
* Hawaii
* Idaho
* Illinois
* Indiana
* Iowa
* Kansas
* Louisiana
* Maine
* Nebraska
* Nevada
* New Hampshire
* New Jersey
* New York
* North Carolina
* Ohio
* Oklahoma
* Oregon
* Pennsylvania
* Tennessee
* Wisconsin

In addition to these states, the District of Columbia also has enacted legislation to regulate the activities and practices of credit repair companies.

Consumer Credit File Rights Under State and Federal Law

Under the Credit Repair Organizations Act any credit repair organization must provide any consumer with the following written statement before any contract agreement between the consumer and the credit repair organization is signed:

Consumer Credit File Rights Under State and Federal Law

You have the right to dispute inaccurate information in your credit report by contacting the credit bureau directly. However, neither you nor any "credit repair" company or credit repair organization has the right to have accurate, current, and verifiable information removed from your credit report. The credit bureau must remove accurate, negative information from your report only if it is over 7 years old. Bankruptcy information can be reported for 10 years.

You have a right to obtain a copy of your credit report from a credit bureau. You may be charged a reasonable fee. There is no fee, however, if you have been turned down for credit, employment, insurance, or a rental dwelling because of information in your credit report within the preceding 60 days. The credit bureau must provide someone to help you interpret the information in your file. You are entitled to receive a free copy of your credit report if you are unemployed and intend to apply for employment in the next 60 days, if you are a recipient of public welfare assistance, or if you have a reason to believe that there is inaccurate information in your credit report due to fraud.

You have a right to sue a credit repair organization that violates the Credit Repair Organization Act. This law prohibits deceptive practices by credit repair organizations.

You have the right to cancel your contract with any credit repair organization for any reason within 3 business days from the date you signed it.

Credit bureaus are required to follow reasonable procedures to ensure that the information they report is accurate. However, mistakes may occur.

You may, on your own, notify a credit bureau in writing that you dispute the accuracy of information in your credit file. The credit bureau must then reinvestigate and modify or remove inaccurate or incomplete information. The credit bureau may not charge any fee for this service. Any pertinent information and copies of all documents you have concerning an error should be given to the credit bureau.

If the credit bureau's reinvestigation does not resolve the dispute to your satisfaction, you may send a brief statement to the credit bureau, to be kept in your file, explaining why you think the record is inaccurate. The credit bureau must include a summary of your statement about disputed information with any report it issues about you.

The Federal Trade Commission regulates credit bureaus and credit repair organizations. For more information contact:

The Public reference Branch
Federal Trade Commission
Washington, D. C. 20580.

Chapter 6

MAINTAINING A GOOD CREDIT RECORD

Once you begin the process of repairing your credit, you'll need to make a plan for keeping your finances in good standing in order to avoid a recurrence of your money troubles. Re-establishing and maintaining good credit should be a top priority. In this chapter, we'll look at some basic ways you can do just that.

Take Charge Of Your Credit

After you've repaired your credit and your money troubles have eased you, like many other consumers before you, may be tempted to "backslide" and fall into the debt trap again. To avoid another financial crisis, you should steer clear of the temptation to overspend. Here are three money management tips that can help you accomplish that goal.

1) Keep track of your spending

* Avoid incidental and impulse purchases. Remember that credit cards are just like loans — you have to pay what you owe. And as you may have already learned the hard way, owing more money than you can repay can damage your credit rating, making it difficult (if not impossible) to finance a car, rent an apartment, get insurance, or even get a job.

* Pay your bills on time, and in full whenever possible. If you don't, you'll end

up paying finance charges on the unpaid balance — and it takes forever to pay off a debt if you just pay the minimum each month.

2) Keep a close eye on your card and your account number.

* Never lend your credit card to anyone because you and only you are responsible for paying the bill. And any problems with the bill can damage your credit rating and ability to get more credit.

* Never sign a blank charge slip. Instead, draw a line through blank spaces on charge slips above the total so the amount cannot be changed.

* Never put your account number on the outside of an envelope or a post card.

* Don't disclose your account number over the phone unless you know you are dealing with a reputable company.

* Carry only the cards you plan on using to help prevent loss or theft.

* If your credit or ATM cards are stolen, report it to the issuers as soon as possible. Many companies have toll-free numbers and 34-hour service to handle such emergencies. Follow up with a letter, including your account number, when you first noticed the card was missing, and the date you first reported the loss.

3) Keep Good Records

* Save all of your receipts. Compare them each month with your each bill that comes in. You should promptly report problems to the company that issued the card. Generally, your statement will provide instructions for disputing a charge.

* If you shop by mail, phone or online, keep copies or printouts with complete details about the transaction, including any warranties, or return and refund policies if you're not satisfied. You should have the company's name, address, phone number, the date of your order, a copy of the order form you sent to the company or a list of the items ordered and their stock codes, the order confirmation codes and the ad or catalog from which you ordered.

What Creditors Look For

When you apply for credit, lenders, such as banks, look for an ability to repay debt and a willingness to do so. In determining those factors, creditors generally use the three C's of credit worthiness: capacity, character and collateral.

* Capacity. Can you repay the debt? To evaluate your ability to repay a debt, creditors ask for employment information, including your occupation, how long you've worked, and your income. They also want to know all about your expenses — how many dependents you have, whether or not you pay alimony or child support, and the amount of your other obligations.

* Character. Will you repay the debt? Creditors will examine your credit history to find out how often you borrow, whether or not you pay your bills on time, and whether you live within your means. They also look for signs of stability, such a show long you've lived at your present address, whether or not you own or rent, and the length of your present employment.

* Collateral. Is the creditor fully protected in the event you fail to repay? Creditors want to know what assets you have that can be used to back up or secure your loan and what sources you have for repaying debt other than income, such as savings, investments, or property.

Generally, creditors use different combinations of the three C's in reaching their decisions whether or not to give you credit. Some creditors set very high standards and other simply don't make certain kinds of loans. Creditors also use different kinds of rating systems. Some rely solely on their own instinct and experience. Others use a "credit-scoring" system (see Chapter 2, "How To Get Your Credit Report") or statistical system to predict whether or not you are a good credit risk. They assign a certain number of points to each of various characteristics that have proved to be reliable indications that a borrower will repay. Your creditworthiness is then rated on this scale.

Considering the Three C's usually results in different creditors reaching different conclusions based on the same set of facts. While one creditor may deem you an acceptable risk, another may deny you a loan based on the same information.

Applying For Credit

When you apply for credit or a personal loan, you generally must choose from three basic types of credit accounts offered by creditors: revolving, charge, and installment accounts.

Revolving Accounts

With this type of account, you pay in full each month or you may choose to make a partial payment based on the outstanding balance. You must pay at least the minimum amount due on a revolving account. Banks, department stores, and oil and gas companies typically offer credit cards based on a revolving credit plan.

Charge Account

With a charge account, you promise to pay the full balance due each month, so you can avoid paying interest charges. Charge cards (not credit cards) and charge accounts with local retail businesses typically require payment on a charge account basis.

Installment Account

In this type of credit agreement, you sign a contract to repay a fixed amount or credit in equal payments over a specific period of time. Automobiles, furniture and major appliances usually are financed this way. Personal loans and mortgage loans are usually paid back in installments, as well.

Getting The Best Deal On A Credit Card

As you can no doubt tell from the flood of credit card offers in your mailbox, no two offers are the same. Fees, charges and benefits vary among credit card issuers, so before you choose a credit card it's a good idea to shop around for the best deal possible. Here are some important things you should consider when choosing a credit card:

* The annual percentage rate (APR). This is a measure of the cost of credit, expressed as a yearly interest rate. You also should check out the card's "periodic rate", too. That's the rate the card issuer applies to your outstanding balance to figure the finance charge for each billing period. For example, let's say

you have an outstanding balance of $2,000, with 18.5 percent interest and a low minimum monthly payment it would take over 11 years to pay off the debt. It would also cost you an additional $1,934 just for interest, which would be almost twice the amount of your original purchase.

* Grace period. You should know how much time you'll have between the date of a purchase and the date interest starts being charged on that purchase. If you get a card with a standard grace period you can avoid finance charges by paying your current balances in full each month. Some issuers no allow a grace period for new purchases even if you don't pay your balance in full every month. However, if there is no grace period, the card issuer will impose a finance charge from the date you use the card or from the date each purchase is posted to your account.

* Annual fees. Many card issuers charge an annual fee just for granting you the "privilege" of credit. Typically, those fees range anywhere from $15 to $55. If you shop around, you can find a card issuer that does not charge an annual fee.

* Transaction fees and other charges. Some credit card issuers charge a fee if you use the card to get a cash advance, if you fail to make a payment on time, or if you exceed your credit limit. Some may charge a flat fee every month even if you don't use the card.

Cash advance fees are especially steep. If you choose a card that allows you to obtain a cash advance, you can expect to pay an interest rate that is much higher than that associated with your normal purchases — as high as 20 percent, with some cards. And that interest often begins to accrue as soon as the transaction is completed, meaning there's no grace period.

* Customer Service. These days, most credit card issuers have 24-hour, toll-free customer service telephone numbers. Many also have customer service available online.

In addition, many credit card issuers also offer a number of other benefits, some with a cost, such as insurance, credit card protection, discounts, rebates, and special merchandise offers. Depending on your needs and how you plan to use the card, you should consider all these factors before choosing a credit card.

How To Deal With Unwanted Credit

If you're like most consumers, you receive an assortment of bills, circulars and other assorted items every day in the mail. Tucked in among these items are pre-approved credit card offers with a line of credit up to $7,500. You study these offers and realize that you never applied for them. The question arises, are you liable for charges made to such a card?

According to the FTC, you are not liable for the unauthorized use of any kind of credit card sent to you without you first having applied for the credit. In fact, under the federal Truth in Lending Act, it's illegal for a creditor of any kind, including banks, department stores and oil companies, to extend credit without either an oral or written application. That includes MasterCard, Visa, and travel and entertainment cards, such as American Express and Diners Club.

The law does say that it is legal for a creditor to issue renewal or replacement credit cards, since your earlier application is on file. A department store or oil company may replace its own card with a full-service Visa or MasterCard. If you activate one of these cards, mistaking if for a replacement card, you could open a credit line you don't rally want. In that event, the previous account is closed when the new account is opened. In order to terminate a credit agreement, you must inform the creditor in writing.

While you can be liable for up to $50 per card for unauthorized use of your legitimate credit cards, there is no liability at all for the misuse of credit for which you never applied.

According to the Better Business Bureau, if you receive an unsolicited credit card you don't want, you should do the following:

* Make a copy of the card, then cut it up.

* Write to the card issuer, stating that you decline the offer and that you wish to have any information that may have been added to your credit report removed immediately.

* Keep a record of the card offer, as well as the letter you sent to the card issuer.

If you do consider keeping the card, don't use it until you've verified all the terms of the agreement with the issuer — that includes the offered credit limit, annual fee, interest rate and length of time for which the rate is guaranteed.

Should You Buy Credit Insurance?

Whenever you apply for a mortgage or personal loan, it's likely you'll be asked if you want to purchase credit insurance. Some creditors include such insurance in their loan proposals. The question is, "is it necessary?" Like any other type of insurance, credit insurance provides protection — it protects the loan on the chance that you can't make your payments. Whether or not it's something you should purchase is a decision you should make based on your individual needs and an understanding of just what you are buying.

The first thing you should understand is that credit insurance usually is optional — you don't have to purchase it from the lender. In fact, the FTC says it's against the law for a lender to deceptively include credit insurance (or any other optional products) in your loan without your knowledge or permission.

There are four basic types of credit insurance offered by most lenders: 1) Credit life insurance, which pays off all or some of your loan if you die; 2) Credit disability insurance, also known as accident and health insurance, which makes payments on the loan if you become ill or injured and can't work; 3) Involuntary unemployment insurance, also known as involuntary loss of income, which makes your loan payments if you lose your job due to no fault of your own, such as a layoff; 4) Credit property insurance, which protects personal property used to secure the loan if destroyed by events, such as theft, accidental or natural disasters.

Before you sign on the dotted line and buy credit insurance from a lender, you should consider your needs, your options, and the rates you're going to pay — which typically are quite high. Once you find out the rates, you may decide you don't need credit insurance after all. The truth is, credit insurance can be an expensive form of insurance. You may get better protection at a much better rate if you buy life insurance than credit insurance. Before deciding to buy credit insurance, you should ask yourself the following questions:

* How much is the premium?

* How will the premium be financed — as part of the loan? If so, it will increase the amount of your loan and you'll pay additional interest, and more for points (if points are on your loan).

* Can you pay monthly instead of financing the entire premium as part of your loan?

* How much lower would your monthly payment be without credit insurance?

* Will the insurance cover the full length of your loan and the full loan amount?

* What are the limits and exclusions on payment of benefits - that is, find out exactly what's covered and what's not.

* Will there be a waiting period before the coverage becomes effective?

* If you have a co-borrower, what coverage does he or she have and at what cost?

* Can you cancel the insurance? If so, what kind of refund is available?

Also, before you sign any loan papers, ask the lender whether the loan includes any charges for voluntary credit insurance. If you don't want credit insurance, tell the lender. If the lender still pressures you to buy insurance, walk away and find another lender. And be sure to review your loan papers to make sure they have been drawn up correctly.

The law says that lenders can't deny you credit if you don't buy optional credit insurance — and if you don't buy it directly from them. If a lender tells you that you can get the loan only if you buy the optional credit insurance, report the company to your state attorney general, your state insurance commissioner, of the FTC.

Using Debit Cards

Despite the increasing number of consumers using debit cards these days, many still don't know all that much about them. Put simply, when you use a debit card, the amount you spend is limited by what you have in your bank account.

While debit cards look like credit cards or ATM cards, they operate like cash or a personal check. When you use a debit card, your money is immediately deducted from your checking or savings account.

There are two basic types of debit transactions, both often residing on the same card that your bank sends you as a replacement for your old ATM card. First of all, there are online transactions you perform at an ATM. You just enter a personal identification card (PIN) and money is electronically transferred from your account exactly as you stipulate. The second type of debit transaction is an offline transaction, in which you present your debit card in a store and it is treated like a credit card sale. The money used to pay for the transaction then is deducted from your checking account, usually within a couple of days.

According to a recent survey sponsored by the National Consumers League, many consumers don't understand their liability limits, and also are confused about protections offered by banks and debit card providers. With that in mind, we suggest that before you use a debit card, you should contact your bank or card issuer and get answers to the following questions:

* What are the liability limits if my debit card is lost or stolen?

* What fees, if any, will I be charged for using my debit card?

* Is there a limit on how much money I can debit pre day, or per month?

* Do I have the same purchase protections with my debit card that I have with a credit card?

* Can I have my photograph shown on my debit card?

* If my debit card is stolen and money is taken out of my account, how soon will the money be replaced by the bank?

Credit And Divorce

Nearly half of all American marriages end in divorce. Besides the obvious emotional difficulties of going through such proceedings, there may be serious financial difficulties, as well. Until fairly recently, the financial problems that typically accompany divorce were mostly a concern for women. Nowadays, with more and more women becoming the major wage earners in their families, men are confronted with divorce-related financial difficulties, as well.

If you've recently been through a divorce, or are considering one, it's a good idea to take a close look at issues involving your credit. Understanding the different kinds of credit accounts opened during marriage may help minimize any potential financial problems that could occur as a result of divorce.

There are two basic types of credit accounts: individual and joint. You can authorize other people to use the account with either. When you apply for credit — whether a charge card or a mortgage loan — you'll be asked to select one type.

Individual Account

When you apply for this type of account, a creditor will consider your income, assets, and credit history. Whether you are married or single, you are solely responsible for paying off the debt. The account will appear on your credit report and also will likely appear on the credit report of anyone you have authorized to use the account. However, if you live in a community property state (Arizona, California, Idaho, Louisiana, New Mexico, Texas, Washington, or Wisconsin), both you and your spouse may be responsible for debts incurred during the marriage. In addition, the individual debts of one spouse may appear on the credit report of the other.

The main advantage of maintaining your own, individual account is that, if you have a good-paying job and are responsible, no one else can negatively effect your credit record (legally, that is). However, if you aren't employed outside the home, work part-time, or have a low-paying job, you may have trouble getting credit without your spouse's income

Joint Accounts

Creditors generally consider the same factors when you apply for a joint account as they do when considering whether or not to open an individual account. It doesn't matter who pays the household bills, both you and your spouse are responsible for seeing that all debts are paid. A creditor who reports the credit history of a joint account to a CRA must report it in both names.

Again, there are both advantages and disadvantages of maintaining joint accounts. For example, an application combing the financial resources of two people with good credit ratings will present a stronger case to a creditor who is granting a loan or issuing a credit card. On the other hand, when two people apply together for credit, each is responsible for the debt. That hold true even if a divorce decree assigns separate debt obligations to each spouse. Former spouses who run up bills and don't pay them can damage their ex-spouse's credit ratings on jointly-held accounts.

Authorized Account "Users"

As noted earlier, if you open an individual account, you may authorize another person to use it. If you name your spouse as the authorized user, a creditor who reports the credit history to a CRA must report it in your spouse's name as well as in yours. In addition, a creditor may report the credit history in the name of any other authorized user.

Typically, user accounts are opened as a matter of convenience. These accounts benefit people who may not otherwise qualify for credit on their own, such as homemakers or students. While these people may use your account and incur added debt, it's important that you understand that you are solely responsible and contractually liable for paying the debt.

What Happens To Your Credit When You Divorce

If you're contemplating divorce or separation, you should pay close attention to the status of your credit accounts. If you and your spouse maintain joint accounts during this time, it's important that you make regular payments so your credit record won't be damaged. As long as there is an outstanding balance on a joint account, both you and your spouse are responsible for it.

If you divorce, you may want to close joint accounts or accounts in which your former spouse was an authorized user. Or you may request that the creditor convert these accounts to individual accounts.

According to the law, a creditor cannot close a joint account because of a change in marital status, but can do so at the request of either spouse. However, a creditor is not required to change joint accounts to individual accounts. The creditor can require you to reapply for credit on an individual basis and then, based on your new application, extend or deny you credit. In the case of a mortgage or home equity loan, a lender is likely to require refinancing to remove a spouse from the obligation.

Steps To Take Before Filing For Divorce

Granted, the emotional strain and stress of divorce can be debilitating, but practical matters, such as finances, must be considered, as well. Here are several steps you can take before filing for divorce that can help you (and your spouse) minimize any potential damage to your credit standing:

* It's essential that you have good credit in your own name. If you don't, try to delay your divorce (if possible) until you can get some individual credit and open a bank account in your own name.

* Review the status of the accounts that you and your spouse are currently using. You should know, for example, whether or not the accounts are joint accounts, authorized-user, or individual.

* If you already either joint or individual credit, you should get a copy of your credit report from each of the big three CRAs and deal with any problems you find in them (see Chapter 3 for information on how to dispute and correct credit report errors).

* Make an effort to pay all bills and credit card debts you share with your spouse from your joint accounts. As soon as the debts are paid, send a letter to each creditor canceling the cards and closing the accounts. Leaving the accounts open will put you at potential financial risk. You may be liable for the balances on any open accounts.

Divorce and Bankruptcy

Bankruptcy, while a possible solution to financial difficulties, is, as we said before, a debt management tool of last resort. It's also important that you understand that you cannot discharge child support or alimony through bankruptcy.

If your spouse or ex-spouse files for bankruptcy relief, he or she will get all of the debt in his/her name discharged or forgiven. In addition, if you still have joint debts and your spouse includes them in his/her bankruptcy, you are then solely responsible for paying off those debts. Obviously, the best advice in this situation, is to consult with your lawyer about how to minimize the potential impact of your spouse's impending bankruptcy on your finances.

The Law Is On Your Side

Throughout the preceding chapters, we've described several important laws that provide specific consumer credit-related rights. And by now you should have a good understanding of your rights under the Fair Credit Reporting Act. To protect your rights and your rebuilt credit, you also should have knowledge and an understanding of your rights under several other federal laws: the Equal Credit Opportunity Act, The Fair Credit Billing Act, the Truth in Lending Act, and the Mail or Telephone Order Merchandise Rule.

Equal Credit Opportunity Act (ECOA)

The ECOA was enacted to ensure that all consumers are given an equal chance to obtain credit. It prohibits credit discrimination on the basis of sex, race, marital status, religion, national origin, age or receipt of public assistance. Now, that doesn't mean that everyone who applies for credit get it. As you know, factors such as income, expenses, debt, and credit history all go into determining an individual's creditworthiness.

The ECOA protects consumers who deal with creditors who regularly extend credit, including banks, small loan and finance companies, retail and department stores, credit card companies, and credit unions. Anyone involved in granting credit of any sort, such as real estate brokers who arrange financing, is covered by this law. Even businesses applying for credit are covered by the ECOA.

When you apply for credit, the ECOA says that a creditor may not:

* Deny you credit based on your race, sex, marital status, religion, age, national origin, or because you receive public assistance.

* Ask you to reveal your sex, race, national origin, or religion. A creditor may ask you to voluntarily provide this information (except for religion) if you're applying for a real estate loan. The information helps federal agencies enforce anti-discrimination laws.

* Ask if you're widowed or divorced. When permitted to ask about marital status, a creditor may only use the terms, married, unmarried, or separated.

* Ask about your marital status if you're applying for a separate, unsecured account.

* Request information about your spouse, except when your spouse is applying with you; your spouse will be allowed to use the account; you rely on the spouse's income or on alimony or child support income from a former spouse; or if you reside in a community property state, such as Arizona, California, Idaho, Louisiana, Nevada, New Mexico, Texas and Washington.

* Ask about your plans for having or raising children.

After you apply for credit, a creditor may not:

* Consider your sex, marital status, race, national origin, or religion.

* Consider whether or not you have a telephone listing in your name. A creditor may, however, consider whether or not you have a phone.

* Consider the race of people who live in the neighborhood where you want to buy, refinance or improve a house with borrowed money.

* Consider you age, unless:

> you're too young to sign contracts, usually younger than 18 years old.;
> you're 62 or older, and the creditor will favor you because of your age;
> it's used to determine the meaning of other factors important to creditworthiness. For example, under a valid credit-scoring system (see Chapter 2) that favors applicants 62 and older, your length of employment might be scored differently, depending on your age.

* Refuse to consider public assistance income the same ways as other income.

* Refuse to consider regular alimony, child support, or separate maintenance payments. A creditor may, however, ask you to prove that you are receiving this income consistently.

The ECOA also gives you the right to:

* Apply for credit under your maiden name, your married name or a combina-

tion.

* Obtain credit without a co-signer, if you meet the creditor's standards.

* Have a co-signer other than your spouse, if a co-signer is necessary.

* Keep your own accounts after you change your name, marital status, reach a certain age, or retire. (Unless the creditor has evidence that you are unwilling or unable to pay).

* Know whether or not your application was accepted or rejected within 30 days of filing a complete application.

* Know why your application was rejected. The creditor must provide a notice that tells you either the specific reasons for your rejection or your right to learn the reasons if you ask within 60 days.

* Find out why you were offered less favorable terms than you applied for - unless you accept the terms.

If you suspect discrimination, you first should lodge a complaint with the creditor. Make it clear that you know the law. If you get no satisfaction, then check with your state attorney general to see if the creditor violated state equal credit opportunity laws. You state may then decide to prosecute the creditor.

Other legal options include:

* Bring a case in federal district court. If you win, you can recover damages, including punitive damages. You also can be awarded compensation for attorney fees and court costs. An attorney can advise you on how to proceed.

* Join with others and file a class action suit.

* Report violations to the appropriate government agency. If you are denied credit, the creditor must give you the name and address of the agency to contact. While some of these agencies don't resolve individual complaints, the information you provide helps them decide which companies to investigate.

Fair Credit Billing Act (FCBA)

The Fair Credit Billing Act applies to "open end" credit accounts, such as credit cards, and revolving charge accounts, such as department store accounts (It doesn't apply to installment contracts — loans or extensions of credit you repay on a fixed schedule). The types of disputes covered under the FCBA include the following "billing errors":

* Unauthorized charges. Federal law limits your responsibility for unauthorized charges to $50;

* Charges that list the wrong date or amount;

* Charges for goods and services you didn't accept or weren't delivered as agreed;

* Math errors;

* Failure to post payments and other credits, such as returns;

* Failure to send bills to your current address - provided that the creditor receives your change of address, in writing, at least 20 days before the billing period ends; and

* Charges for which you ask for an explanation or written proof of purchase along with a claimed error or request for clarification.

To take advantage of the FCBA's protections, you'll need to send a letter to the creditor's "billing inquiries" department (see Chapter 8, "Letters") and not the address for sending your payments, and include your name, address, account number and a description of the billing error. Send your letter so that it reaches the creditor within 60 days after the first bill containing the error was mailed to you.

As with other credit-related letters, you should send this letter by certified mail, return receipt requested, so that you have proof of what the creditor received. And again, include copies of sales slips or other documents that support your position. The creditor is required to acknowledge your complaint in writing within 30 days after receiving it, unless the problem has been resolved. Under the law, the creditor must resolve the billing dispute with two billing cycles (but not more than 90 days) after receiving your letter.

While the creditor is investigating your claim, you may withhold payment on the disputed amount (and related charges). However, you must pay any part of the bill not in question, including any finance charges on the disputed amount. In the meantime, the creditor may not take any legal or other action to collect the disputed amount and the related charges (including finance charges) during the investigation. Although your account cannot be closed or restricted, the disputed amount may be applied against your credit limit.

In addition, the creditor may not threaten your credit rating or report you as delinquent while your bill is in dispute. However, the creditor may report that you are challenging your bill.

What Happens If Your Bill Is incorrect?

If your bill does contain an error, the creditor must explain to you — in writing - the corrections that will be made to your account. In addition to crediting your account, the creditor must remove all finance charges, late fees or other charges related to the error.
Should the creditor determine that you owe a portion of the disputed amount, you must get a written explanation. You have the right to request copies of documents proving you owe the money.

What Happens If Your Bill Is Correct?

If you are wrong and the creditor's investigation determines that your bill is correct, you must be told promptly and in writing exactly how much you owe and why. You may request copies of all relevant documents. If this happens, you'll owe the disputed amount, plus any finance charges that accumulated while the amount was in dispute. You also may have to pay the minimum amount you missed paying because of the dispute. .

You Have The Right To Disagree

If you disagree with the results of the creditor's investigation, you may write to the creditor, but you must do so within 10 days after receiving the explanation, and you must state that you refuse to pay the disputed amount. At this point, the creditor may begin collection proceedings. However, if the creditor reports you to a credit reporting agency as being delinquent, your credit report also must state that you don't think you owe the money. In addition, the creditor must tell you who gets these reports.

If the Creditor Fails To Follow FCBA Procedure

A creditor who fails to follow the FCBA mandated settlement procedure may not collect the amount in dispute, or any related finance charges, up to $50, even if the bill turns out to be correct. For example, if a creditor acknowledges your complaint in 40 days — 10 days too late — or takes more than two billing cycles to resolve a dispute, the penalty applies. The penalty also applies if a creditor threatens to report — or improperly reports - your failure to pay anyone during the dispute period.

Disputes About The Quality of Goods

If you use your credit card to purchase merchandise that turns out to be defective, damaged or of poor quality, the "billing errors" dispute procedure under the FCBA does not apply. However, if you buy unsatisfactory goods or services with a credit or charge card, you can take the same legal actions against the card issuer as you can take under state law against the seller.

To take advantage of the FCBA protection regarding the quality of goods or services, you must have made a purchase (for more than $50) in your home state or within 100 miles of your current billing address. You also must make a good faith effort to first resolve the dispute with the seller.

Truth in Lending Act (TLA)

To make informed credit decisions, you need to be able to compare the cost of borrowing to paying cash. You also need to be able to compare the costs of borrowing from different lenders. To ensure that consumers can do that, the federal government enacted the Truth in Lending Act. The TLA requires that lenders disclose certain costs and terms. You usually get these disclosures when you receive an application for a loan. You'll also get additional disclosures before the account is opened.

Under the TLA, lenders are required to disclose terms and costs of all loan plans, including the interest rate you will be charged; annual percentage rate, points and fees; the total of the principal amount being financed; payment due date and terms, including any balloon payment and late payment fees; any grace period that may be applicable; annual or one-time service fees; and any pre-payment penalties. Generally, neither the lender no anyone else may charge a fee until you have received this disclosure information.

Lenders who advertise must meet Truth in Lending Act disclosure requirements regarding the loan rate and terms. These requirements include:

* The lender must make specific credit terms in an ad available to all applicants.

* When an advertisement includes a specific rate, it must state the rate as an annual percentage rate percentage rate (APR) using that exact term. This rate takes into account all additional costs incurred, including fees and points, in the first year of the loan.

* The advertisement must state whether or not the APR may be increased after the loan is closed.

* No other rate is allowed to appear in the advertisement, except a simple annual rate or periodic rate that is applied to an unpaid balance. It may be stated in conjunction with, but not more prominently than the APR.

The TLA also provides consumers with certain protections against lost or stolen credit cards. It limits your liability should you lose one or more credit cards or if they are stolen to $50. The only requirement is that you notify the appropriate credit card company as soon as you are aware of the loss or theft. Once you do that, it doesn't matter how much unauthorized spending occurs with your credit card — your liability is no more than $50.

If a creditor fails to disclose information required under the TLA, or gives inaccurate information, or otherwise violates the law, you as an individual consumer have the right to sue for actual damages and any money loss you suffer. You also can sue for twice the finance charge in the case of certain credit disclosures. In any case, the smallest amount the court may award you is if you win is $100, and the most is $1,000. In addition, you are entitled to reimbursement for court costs and attorney's fees.

The Mail or Telephone Order Merchandise Rule

This rule covers merchandise you order by mail, telephone, computer and fax. It requires merchants to have a reasonable basis for claiming they can ship an order within a certain time.

Shipping Date

* By law, a merchant must ship your order within the time stated in its advertisements or over the phone. If the merchant doesn't promise a shipping date, you can expect it to ship your order within 30 days.

* The shipment "clock" begins when the merchant receives a "properly completed order." Such an order includes your name, address and payment (check, money order or authorization to charge an existing credit account).

* If the merchant doesn't promise a shipping date and you are applying for credit to pay for your purchase, the merchant has an additional 20 days (50 days total) to establish the account and ship the merchandise.

What About Delays?

If the merchant is not able to ship within the promised time, it must notify you by mail, telephone, or email, and give you a revised shipping date. It also must give you the option of canceling for a full refund or accept the new shipping date. The merchant also must give you some way to exercise the cancellation option for free. For example, it may send you a prepaid reply card or provide a toll-free telephone number.

Contacts for Resolving Disputes

If you have problems with your purchase and can not get satisfaction by contacting the company, you may find the following resources helpful;

* State and local consumer protection offices. Contact the offices in your home state and where the company is located.

* The Direct Marketing Association (DMA): Write:
DMA Mail Order Action Line
1111 19th Street, N.W. , Suite 1100
Washington, DC 20036-3603

* Postal Inspectors. Call your local post office and ask for the "Inspector-in-Charge".

Chapter 7

How To Protect Your Credit And Financial Privacy

You may not realize it, but every day you are sharing personal and financial information about yourself with other people. It happens whenever you write a check at the grocery store, charge tickets to a ball game, rent a car, mail your tax returns, buy something online, call home on your cell phone, schedule a doctor's appointment or apply for a credit card. Every one of these and similar transactions requires you to share information, such as your bank and credit card account numbers; your income; your Social Security number (SSN); or your name, address and phone numbers.

While most recipients of that information are honest businesses — getting and giving legitimate information, there are others who use your information for dishonest purposes.

That's why it's essential that you find out just what happens to the personal information you provide to companies, marketers and government agencies. Generally, these companies and agencies use your information simply to process your order; to tell you about their products, services or promotions; or to share with others within their rights under the law.

The problem is that there are other unscrupulous individuals, like identity thieves, who want your information to commit fraud. Consumers who are targeted by identity thieves usually aren't even aware they've been victimized — until, that is, the thieves fail to pay the bills or repay the loans. Then collection agencies begin pursuing the consumers to cover debts they didn't even know they had. And when that happens, a consumer's credit rating can take a serious hit.

Unfortunately, all a creditor has to say is that you were late or delinquent in your payments and it goes on your credit record. You're assumed guilty until proven innocent. It's your responsibility to prove to a creditor's satisfaction that you were in fact, not late and that you weren't even aware someone was using your account.

The sad truth is that your credit and financial well-being is at risk every day, simply by virtue of you having and using credit. The importance of protecting your credit and financial privacy in today's world cannot be understated. In this chapter we will provide you with information on how to minimize the potential risk of using credit and how to protect your financial identity.

Credit Card Loss Protection Offers

If the phone rings, it just may be another telephone scam artists after your money. One of the latest scams involves the offer via the telephone of credit card loss protection insurance. Simply put, these telephone con artists are lying to get people to buy worthless credit card loss protection insurance programs. The best credit card loss insurance you have is free. Put more simply, if you didn't authorize a charge on your credit card, you don't have to pay it. Just follow your credit card issuer's procedures for disputing charges you haven't authorized. According to the FTC, your liability for unauthorized charges is $50, no more (see Chapter 5).

The FTC also says that worthless credit card loss protection offers are popular among fraudulent promoters who are trying to exploit consumers' uncertainty, in tough economic times. As a result, the agency cautions consumers to avoid doing business with callers who claim that:

* You're liable for more than $50 in unauthorized charges on your credit account;

* You need credit card loss protection because computer hackers can access your credit card number and charge thousands of dollars to you account;

* A computer bug could make it easy for crooks to place unauthorized charges on your credit card account, and;

* They're from the "security department" and want to activate the protection feature on your credit card.

Your best defense against this credit scam is to avoid giving out personal information, including your credit card or bank account number(s) over the phone or online unless you are familiar with the business that's asking you for the information. Crooks can use your personal information to commit fraud, such as identity theft. An all-too-common example is when an identity thief uses your personal information to open a credit card account in your name.

You can get more information about how to protect yourself against credit card theft by calling the FTC toll-free, at 1-877-FTC-HELP (1-877-382-4357), or visit www.ftc.gov to get the free publications, such as, "Credit, ATM and Debit Cards: What to do if They're Lost or Stolen".

Identity Theft

Identity theft happens when someone uses your name or personal information, such as your Social Security number, driver's license number, credit card number, telephone number or other account numbers, without your permission. Identity thieves use this information to open credit accounts, bank accounts, telephone service accounts, and make major purchases, all in your name. Information can be used to take over your existing accounts, or to open new accounts. Identity theft is becoming more and more common and can result in damage to your credit rating and ultimately in denials of credit and job offers.

In many cases, identity theft begins with the loss or theft of a wallet or purse. However, there are many other ways that crooks can get and use your personal information in order to commit identity theft. For example, you receive an email from what appears to be your Internet Service provider (ISP). The message requests that you update the information your ISP has on file about you - your name, credit card number, bank account number, etc.— by replying to the email or going to a specific Web site address to provide the information. However, neither he message nor the Web site address is from your ISP. They belong to a con artist who wants to get your information in order to steal your identity.

Protecting Your Identity

While there is no guarantee that your identity will never be stolen, there are some things you can do to minimize the risk. Below are several tips on how to protect your identity:

* Don't give out your Social Security number to people or companies that you do not know.

* Before disclosing any personal information, make sure you know why it is required and how it will be used.

* Shred information you no longer need that contains personally identifiable information and account numbers. For example, credit card receipts, billing statements and pre-approved credit offers should be shredded before you discard them.

* Guard your mail from theft. Promptly remove your incoming mail from your mailbox and place outgoing mail in the post office collection boxes. Install a locking mailbox if mail theft is a problem in your neighborhood.

* Keep the personal information you have at home and at work in a safe place.

* Do not carry extra credit cards, your birth certificate or passport, or other cards that display your Social Security number in your wallet or purse, except when necessary.

* Create unique passwords on your banking and brokerage accounts.

* Get a copy of your credit report from each of the big three CRAs at least once a year (see Chapter 2). Review the reports to make sure that no one else is using your identity to open new accounts or to use your existing accounts.

What To Do If You Are A Victim Of Identity Theft

If you think you have been victimized by identity theft, you should take the following steps, immediately:

1) Contact the fraud departments of each of the big three credit bureaus. Request that a "fraud alert" be placed on your file and include a statement that the creditors must get your permission before any new accounts are opened in your name. Get a copy of your credit report from each bureau so that you can dispute any inaccurate information. Once identity theft has occurred, you should check your reports at least every six months.

2) Contact all the creditors involved. Let them know that your accounts may have been used without your permission, or that new accounts have been opened in your name. If your accounts have been used fraudulently, ask that new cards and account numbers be issued to you. Check your billing statements carefully and report any fraudulent activity immediately. Many banks and creditors will accept the "ID Theft Affidavit" available online at www.consumer.gov/idtheft, to dispute the fraudulent charges.

3) File a police report. Get a copy of the report to submit to your creditors and others that may require proof of a crime.

4) Contact the Federal Trade Commission. The FTC provides useful information to identity theft victims and maintains a database of identity theft cases for use by law enforcement agencies. You can file a report with the FTC by calling the agency's Identity Theft Hotline: 1-877-IDTHEFT (438-4388); by mail, Identity Theft Clearinghouse, Federal Trade Commission, 600 Pennsylvania Avenue, N.W., Washington, DC 20580; or online at www.consumer.gov/idtheft. You also may request for a free copy of the FTC publication, "ID Theft, When Bad Things Happen To Your Good Name".

5) Keep a detailed record of all your contacts. Start a file with copies of your credit reports, the police report, any correspondence, and copies of disputed bills. You also may find it helpful to keep a log of your conversations with creditors, law enforcement officials, and other relevant parties. Follow up all phone calls in writing and send all correspondence certified, return receipt requested.

Re-taking Control Of Your Identity

While an identity thief can cause serious problems with your personal finances, there are some things you can do to take control of the situation and reclaim your identity. Here are some tips for taking control of the most common types of identity theft:

* A crime has been committed if an identity thief has stolen your mail for access to new credit cards, bank and credit card statements, pre-approved credit offers and tax information or falsified change-of-address forms. Report such a crime to your local postal inspector.

* If you discover that an identity thief has changed the billing address on an existing credit card account, close the account immediately. When you open a new account, ask that a password be used before any inquiries or changes can be made on the account. You should avoid using easily available password information like your mother's maiden name, your birth date, the last four digits of your Social Security number, or a series of consecutive numbers. Also avoid the same information and numbers when you create a Personal Identification Number (PIN).

* If you're sure that someone has accessed your bank accounts, checking account or ATM card, close those accounts immediately. When you open new accounts, again insist on password-only access. If your checks have been stolen or misused, stop payment. If your ATM card has been lost, stolen or otherwise compromised, cancel the card and get another with a new PIN.

* If an identity thief has established new phone or wireless service in your name and is making unauthorized calls that appear to come from - and are billed to - your cellular phone, or is using your calling card and PIN, contact your service provider immediately to cancel the account and calling card. Get new accounts and new PINS.

* If you have reason to believe that someone is using your Social Security number when applying for a job, get in touch with the Social Security Administration (SSA) to verify the accuracy of your reported earnings and that that your name is reported correctly. Call the SSA at 1-800-772-1213 to check your Social Security Statement.

In addition, the SSA may issue you a new Social Security number at your request, if the problems brought on by the identity theft persist. You should consider this option carefully. That's because a new Social Security number may not resolve your identity theft problems, and may actually create new problems. For example, a new SSN does not necessarily ensure a new credit record because credit bureaus may combine the credit records for your old SSN with those from your new SSN. Even if the old credit information is not associated with your new SSN, the absence of any credit history under your new SSN may make it more difficult for you to get credit. In addition, there's no guarantee that a new SSN won't also be misused by an identity thief.

If you think that your name or your SSN is being used by an identity thief to get a driver's license, report it to your Department of Motor Vehicles. Also, if your state uses your SSN as your driver's license number, ask to substitute another number.

Shopping Safely On The Internet

The impressive growth of the Internet over the past few years has brought with it a whole new set of privacy issues, especially for the millions of consumers now shopping online. While it is undisputed that shopping online offers lots of benefits that you won't find shopping in a store or by mail — the Internet is open 24/7, and bargains can be numerous online - shopping on the Internet is no less safe than shopping in a store or by mail.

Security on the Internet is an issue that all consumers should be aware of. Here are several tips that can help ensure that you protect both your credit and your financial privacy when shopping online:

1) Use a secure browser. A browser is Internet-speak for the software you use to navigate online. First of all, your browser should comply with industry security standards, such as Secure Sockets Layer (SSL). These standards scramble the purchase information you send over the Internet, helping to make your transactions secure. Most computers come with a browser already installed. You also can download some browsers for free over the Internet.

2) Shop with companies you know and trust. One of the problems with shopping on the Internet is that anyone can set up shop online under almost any name. If you're not familiar with a merchant, ask for a paper catalog or brochure to get as better idea of their merchandise and services. Also, be aware of the company's refund and return policies before you place an order. This information should be posted on the company's Web site.

3) Make sure your passwords are kept private. Use your imagination and be creative when you establish a password, and never give it to anyone — even your most trusted friend. When creating a new password, it's best to avoid using a telephone number, birth date, or portion of your Social Security number. Instead, you should use a combination of numbers, letters, and symbols.

3) Always pay by credit or charge card. If you pay by credit or charge card online, your transaction will be protected by the Fair Credit Billing Act (see Chapter 6 for a detailed explanation of this law). Under this law, consumers have the right to dispute charges under certain circumstances and temporarily withhold payment while the creditor is investigating the disputed charges. If you experience unauthorized use of your credit or charge card, you generally are held liable only for the first $50 in charges. Some companies offer an online shopping guarantee that ensures that you will not be held responsible for any unauthorized charges made online. Other cards may provide additional warranty, return and/or purchase protection benefits.

4) Keep a record of all your online transactions. Be sure to print a copy of your purchase order and confirmation number for your records. You also should be familiar with the Mail/Telephone Order Merchandise Rule (see Chapter 6), which covers online orders. It says that unless stated otherwise, merchandise must be delivered within 30 days; and if there are delays, the company must notify you.

5) Pay your bills online. This may be scary at first, but there are many companies that let you pay your bills and check your account status online. Before you sign up for any such service, you should evaluate how the company secures your financial and personal information. Many companies explain their security procedures on their web site. If you don't see a company's security description, call or email the company and ask about their online security.

Protecting Your Privacy On The Internet

Today's technology provides companies with the ability to collect information about you and potentially give that information to others. While it's true that the Internet can serve as a powerful tool for accessing all sorts of information, products and services, you should take extra care to safeguard your privacy online by following some common sense tips.

* Keep your personal information private. Don't disclose personal information, such as your address, telephone number, SSN or email address, unless you know who's collecting the information, why they're collecting it and how they'll use it.

* Look for a company's online privacy policy. Most companies with privacy

policies post them on their Web sites. A privacy policy should disclose what information is being collected on the Web site and how that information is being used. Before you provide a company with personal information, check its privacy policy. If you can't find a policy, send an email or written message to the Web site and ask about its policy and request that it be posted on the site.

* Make the right choices. Mont companies doing business online give you a choice on their Web site as to whether and how your personal information is used. These companies allow you to decline — or "opt out" of — having personal information, such as your email address, used for marketing purposes or shared with other companies. Look for this choice as part of the company's privacy policy.

If you have concerns or questions about a company's privacy policy, first contact that company directly. If you still have questions about your privacy rights in dealing with a financial company, you can contact the federal or state agency that oversees what type of company. A list of contacts is provided below:

* Board of Governors of the Federal System

This agency regulates state-chartered banks that are members of the Federal Reserve System, bank holding coOmpanies, and branch of foreign banks. Contact:

Division of Consumer and Community Affairs, Stop 801
20theand C Streets, NW
Washington, DC 20551
1-202-452-3693; www.federalreserve.gov

* Commodity Futures Trading Commission

This agency regulates commodity brokers, commodity trading advisors, commodity pools, and introducing brokers. Write to:

Privacy Officer, Office of Chief Counsel
Division of Trading and Markets
Three Lafayette Center

1155 21ST Street, NW
Washington, DC 20581
1-202-418-5430; www.cftc.gov

*** Federal Deposit Insurance Corporation**

The FDIC regulates state-chartered banks that are not members of the Federal Reserve System.

Division of Compliance and Consumer Affairs
550 17th Street, NW
Washington, DC 20429
1-877-ASK-FDIC or 1-877-275-3342; www.fdic.gov

*** Federal Trade Commission**

The FTC regulates any financial company not covered by the other federal regulators, such as mortgage brokers, tax and investment services, finance companies, credit bureaus, nonblank lenders, auto dealers, leasing companies, appraisers, real estate settlement services, credit counseling services, and collection agency services.

Consumer Response Center
600 Pennsylvania Ave, NW
Washington, DC 20580
1-877-FTC-HELP or 1-877-382-4357 toll-free; www.ftc.gov

* National Credit Union Administration

The NCUA regulates federally chartered credit unions. Write to;

Office of Public AND Congressional Affairs
1775 Duke Street
Alexandria, VA 22314-3428
1-703-518-6330; www.ncua.gov

*** Office of the Comptroller of the Currency**

This agency regulates national banks, District of Columbia Banks, federal branches and federal agencies of foreign banks, and subsidiaries of such companies. These typically include banks with "national" or "N.A." in their names.

Customer Assistance Group
1301 McKinney Street
Suite 3710
Houston, TX 77010
1-800-613-6743 (toll-free); www.occ.treas.gov

* Office of thrift Supervision

The Office of Thrift Supervision regulates federal savings and loan associations and federal savings banks.

Consumer Programs
1700 G Street, NW
Washington, DC 206552
1-800-842-6929 (toll-free); www.treas.gov

* Securities and Exchange Commission

The SEC regulates brokerage firms, mutual fund companies and investment advisors.

Office of Investor Education and Assistance
450 5TH Street, NW
Washington, DC 20549-0213
1-202-942-9634; www.sec.gov/complaint.shtml

Federal Laws That Protect Your Personal Privacy

There are two main federal laws, which cover different aspects of how companies can share your financial information. The Fair Credit Reporting Act protects the privacy of certain information credit reporting agencies. As you learned in an earlier chapter, CRAs gather and provide information about you, such as whether or not you pay your bills on time or have filed for bankruptcy, to creditors and other businesses. Under the law, credit bureaus and other CRAs can release your information only to those third parties that have certified that they have a purpose permitted by the FCRA to obtain your consumer credit report, such as to evaluate your application for credit, or employment, or to rent you an apartment.

After a financial company receives your credit report from a CRA, it may want to "share" that information with an affiliate — either a parent company or a subsidiary. Under the FCRA, however, if the financial company plans to share certain information — from your credit report or your credit application — with its affiliates, it usually will notify you beforehand and give you an opportunity to "opt out". The notice you receive in this instance is likely to be included in the privacy notice you get from the financial company under the relatively new Gramm-Leach-Bliley Act.

This act requires financial companies to tell you about their policies concerning the privacy of your personal financial information. There are a few exceptions, but the law does limit the ability of financial companies to share your personal information with certain non-affiliates, which are companies that are unrelated to your financial company. Such companies may include:

* Service providers - companies hired by your financial company to perform a specific service like printing your checks.

* Joint marketers - companies that have an agreement with your financial company to offer you other financial products or services.

* Other third-party non-affiliates - this could include companies that may want access to your financial company's mailing list to tell you about other products and services.

According to the Gramm-Leach-Bliley Act, your financial company can provide your personal information to non-affiliated service providers including joint marketers. However, before it shares your information with other third-party non -affiliates (excluding the above exceptions) your financial company is required to explain to you its information sharing practices and give you the opportunity to opt out.

Privacy Notices You May Receive

> Initial Privacy Notice. This is usually the first privacy notice you receive when you open an account or become a customer of a financial company. If you open an account over the phone, however, and you agree, the company may send you a privacy notice at a later time.

> Annual Privacy Notice. Each financial company that you have a continuing relationship with, such as your credit card company, the bank where you have a checking account, or a company that services you loan, must send you a notice of its privacy policy once a year.

> Notices of Changes in Privacy Policy. When a company changes its privacy policy, it must send you a revised privacy notice or tell you about the changes in the company's next annual notice.

A privacy notice also may be included with your monthly statement or bill, or it may be sent to you in a separate mailing. If you agree to electronic delivery from an Internet financial company, the notice may be sent to you by e-mail or it may be made available to you on the company's Web site.

Unfortunately, many people don't take the time to read these notices and instead toss them into the wastebasket. If your privacy is important to you, these notices can provide important information. When you receive them, you should first of all, read them carefully. Then, if you have any questions about a company's privacy policy, contact the company directly.

If you decide to opt out, follow the instructions provided in the privacy notice and, if necessary, shop around for a financial company with a privacy policy more to your liking.

If after contacting a company about its privacy policy you still have questions or concerns about your privacy rights, you should contact the federal or state agency regulates that type of company (see the list of regulatory agencies listed earlier in this chapter).

More Options For "Opting Out"

The American economy generates an enormous amount of data. Most uses of that information are from honest, legitimate businesses — getting and giving legitimate information. Even with all the benefits of the "information age", you still may want to limit the amount of personal information you share. And many organizations are now giving you the choice to do just that. For example, many companies and information gathering organizations feature an "opt-out" choice that limits the information shared with others or used for promotional purposes. Opting out allows you to cut down on the number of unsolicited telemarketing calls, promotional mail and spam emails that you receive.

In an earlier chapter you learned how to opt-out of the marketing lists of the big three credit reporting agencies: Equifax, Experian and TransUnion. You also can learn more about the options you have for protecting your personal information by contacting the following organizations:

*** Department of Motor Vehicles**

The Drivers Privacy Protection Act forbids states from distributing personal information to direct marketers. It does allow sharing of personal information with law enforcement officials, courts, government agencies, private investigators, insurance underwriters and similar businesses. Check with your sate DMV to find out more, or visit www.ftc.gov/privacy/protect.htm#Motor

*** Direct Marketers**

The Direct Marketing Association (DMA) offers the Mail and Telephone Preference Services, which allow you to opt out or receiving direct mail marketing and telemarketing calls from many national companies for five years.

If you register with these services, your name will be put on a "delete" file that is updated four times a year and made available to direct-mail and telephone marketers. Two to three months after your name is entered into the quarterly file, you should begin to notice that you are getting a fewer number of solicitations. However, your registration with these services will not stop mailings or calls from organizations registered with the DMA's Mail and Telephone Preference Services.

You can have your name deleted from many direct mail or telemarketing lists by writing your own letter or by using the sample letter provided in Chapter 8 of this book. Mail your letter to:

Direct Marketing Association
Mail Preference Service

PO Box 643
Carmel, NY 10512

Or you can go online at www.the-dma.org/consumers/offmailinglist.html

For telemarketing:

Direct Marketing Association
Telephone Preference Service
PO Box 1559
Carmel, NY 10512
You also can go online at: www.the-dma.org/consumers/offtelephonelist.html

Some states also maintain their own "Don Not Call" lists. For more information about these visit www.the-sma.org/government/donnotcalllists.html

For E-mail

The DMA offers a relatively new EMail Preference Service to help consumers reduce the amount of unsolicited commercial emails. To "opt-out" of receiving unsolicited commercial email, use the Direct Marketing Association's online form at www.e-mps.org. Your online request will remain in effect for one year.

Chapter 8

Letters

This chapter features 20 sample letters (and brief explanations of each letter) you may use for a variety of credit-related circumstances. While you may use these letter "as is", you also may customize them to fit your own circumstances by altering the wording and layout. You also should send all letters by certified mail, return receipt requested, so you have proof of what was actually received by a creditor, CRA, etc. It's also a good idea that you use these letters inserted on your own personal stationary or letterhead.

We've also included in this chapter, following the letters, a sample Credit Information Dispute Form. You may use this form to dispute any of the items on your credit report.

1) Letter Requesting Credit Report

The FCRA says that you must be told what's in your credit file and have any errors corrected. To that end, you should do the following:

If a lender refuses you credit because of unfavorable information in your credit report, you have a right to get the name and address of the agency that keeps your report. Then, you may either request information — that is, a copy of your credit report - from the credit bureau by mail or in person. While you may not receive and exact copy of the file, you will at least learn what's in the report. The law also says that the credit bureau must help you interpret the data in your report because it's raw data that may be somewhat difficult to analyze. If you are questioning a credit refusal made within the past 60 days, the CRA is not allowed to charge a fee for giving you the information. Otherwise, you may be charged up to $9 for a copy of your report. When sending a written request for a copy of your credit report, such as the same letter provided in this chapter, be sure to include a check or money order for the cost of the report, if applicable.

2) Letter Disputing Credit Report

If, after receiving a copy of your credit report, you discover that it is inaccurate or incomplete, you have the right to dispute the errors. When you notify the CRA about an error in your report, it generally must investigate and resolve the dispute within 30 days after receiving your letter of dispute. The bureau then will contact the creditor who supplied the information and remove or correct any information that is incomplete or inaccurate from your credit report. Your letter of dispute must ask for a reinvestigation of the item(s) you dispute, as well an explanation of why the information is in error. The letter also should request the CRA to delete or correct the disputed information.

3) Follow up Request For Reinvestigation

Once a CRA receives your letter disputing information in your credit report, it must reinvestigate the items in questioning question — usually within 30 days — unless it considers your dispute frivolous. When the reinvestigation is complete, the CRA must give you the written results and a free copy of the report if the dispute results in a change. If, after 30 days following the CRAs receipt of your letter disputing your credit report, you have not received any response from the CRA, you may follow-up your initial request for reinvestigation with another letter. Your second letter, should be slightly more forceful than your first, and you should remind the CRA that Under the FCRA, it is required to respond with a "reasonable amount of time" (typically 30 days).

4) Letter Disputing Reinvestigation Findings

The result of your letter of dispute requesting a reinvestigation of certain inaccurate items in your credit report, may not turn out in your favor. The CRA may decide that the items you dispute are indeed correct and not changeable. While the CRA is required to notify you by mail, you have the right to disagree with its findings. In that event, you may request the CRA to re-investigate their findings and supply the name of the company which verifies the findings so you may contact the creditor directly. Your letter disputing reinvestigation findings should explain why you disagree with the CRA and provide any supporting evidence which may bolster your claim.

5) Notice of Intent To File Formal Federal Trade Commission Complaint

The Federal Trade Commission works for consumers to prevent fraudulent, deceptive and unfair business practices in the marketplace and to provide specific information to help consumers avoid them. And while the FTC cannot act as your lawyer in private disputes with companies and organizations, information about your experiences and concerns is essential to the enforcement of the FCRA. In some cases, a letter threatening a company with the filing of a formal complaint against them with the FTC, can work in your favor. In the case of an unresponsive CRA, it can lead them to speeding up the reinvestigation you originally requested.

6) Formal Complaint Letter To The Federal Trade Commission

If you still do not receive a satisfactory response, you should carry through with your threat to file a formal complaint with the FTC. Your formal complaint should include your name, address and a brief, but thorough description of your complaint against a specific company. As always, you should include any supporting evidence that may help prove your claim.

7) Letter Requesting Addition of Accounts

Upon review of your credit report, you may find that it doesn't list all of your credit accounts. While most major credit accounts will appear in your credit file, not all creditors furnish CRAs with account information. If you wish omitted open accounts to be added to your credit file, you must send a letter to the CRA requesting addition of such accounts. You should include copies of recent statements or other verification of the accounts you want added to your report.

8) Letter With 100 Word Statement

In accordance with the FCRA, you are entitled to add short statements to your credit report explaining certain items in your report. In that regard, if you have any negative but accurate items in your credit report, you should include a short statement explaining why they are there —- loss of job, unexpected medical bills, divorce, etc. The FCRA says you can add a 100-word statement per line item but, you should only send one letter per entry to ensure that the CRA places in your credit report. Future reports to creditors must include this statement or a summary of it.

9) Letter Requesting Separate Credit Report

Whether you are divorced, separated or married, you are entitled to your own credit report. A separated report is beneficial, especially if the person with whom your report is merged has bad debt, which is not in your name. Even if you both have bad debt, establishing separate files can be mutually beneficial because individually, each has less bad credit to deal with. If you wish to remove a spouse's name from your credit report, you should send a letter similar to the "Requesting Separate Credit Report" letter provided in this chapter.

10) Letter Requesting Merger Of Spouse's Credit Report

If you're married, you have the right to merge credit reports. Such a merger can be beneficial if one of you has very limited or "slightly blemished" credit and the other an excellent credit history. To effect a merger, you should send a letter requesting such action to each of the three main CRAs.

11) Letter To Original Creditor Regarding Dispute of Credit Report

When you send a letter to a CRA disputing items in your credit report, and you receive notice that a creditor has verified the information as accurate and/or complete, you have the right to contact the creditor directly regarding the dispute. Your letter to the creditor should provide the name of the CRA which has your disputed file, an explanation of the error, and support documentation backing up your claim.

12) Letter To A Creditor Regarding A Billing Error

As a consumer, you have certain rights under the Fair Credit Billing Act. Among those, is the right to dispute "billing errors" on your account(s). To take advantage of the FCBA's protection, you must write to the creditor at the address given for "billing inquiries" (not the address for sending your payments), and include your name, address, account number and a brief, but clear description of the billing error. You must send your letter so that it reaches the creditor within 60 days after the first bill containing the error was mailed to you.

13) Letter Closing Account With A Creditor

When you wish to close an account with a creditor, you may send a letter, such as the sample included in this chapter, requesting that the account be closed. This letter need not be lengthy or require an in depth explanation. Simply notify the creditor that you wish to close a specific account. In clued your name, address and the number of the account that you wish to close.

14) Letter To A Requesting Payment Plan

If you are having difficulty meeting certain obligations, you may contact the creditor directly and request a payment plan that you can realistically afford. Your letter should contain a brief explanation of your financial difficulties and why you cannot meet the payment plan in the original agreement. You also should explain that you do intend to pay the amount owed in full, but it will require making reduced monthly payments.

Your new payment plan proposal also should include a request that the creditor report the new payment plan to each of the three major CRAs.

15) Letter Requesting To Opt Out

Creditors and insurers may use CRA information as a basis for sending you unsolicited offers. By law, these offers must include a toll-free number for your to call if you want to remove your name and address from lists for two years (opt out). You also can send a written opt out request to each of the three major CRAs (see Chapter 3).

16) Notice To Put Name On "Do Not Call" List

Under the federal government's new Telemarketing Sales Rule, you have the right to protection from deceptive and abusive telemarketing acts and practices, as well as from unwanted late-night telemarketing calls. If a telemarketer violates these rights, you may send a written complaint and request to be put on a company's "do not call" list. Your letter should include detailed information about the unwanted telemarketing calls you have been receiving, followed by your request that your name be added to the company "do not call list."

17) Creditor Harassment Complaint Letter

The Fair Debt Collection Act prohibits collection agencies from engaging in certain activities to collect debt. For example, a collection agency may not contact a debtor before 8 a.m. or after 9 p.m. nor at a place of work if the collection agency knows calls are not permitted. In addition, a debt collector may not oppress, abuse, threaten, or use obscene language. This letter serves to notify a creditor that a collection agency it has engaged to collect a debt is in violation of the FDCA. (The complete text of the FDCA can be found in Appendix D.)

18) Letter To Request Cessation Of All Contact From A Creditor

Under the FDCA, you have the right to demand that a creditor cease and desist all contact with you. By law, all communication from the creditor must cease at that time except to notify you of other legal actions. You should understand that send such a letter may force a creditor into take another course of action — usually legal action — because you have blocked all communication.

19) Letter To Creditor Regarding Unauthorized Credit Inquiry

The Fair Credit Reporting Act allows only authorized inquiries to appear on a consumer credit report. Authorized inquires are allowed only to people who have a legitimate business need, as recognized by the law. For example, under the FCRA a company is allowed to check your credit file if you apply for credit, insurance, or employment. If you have reason to believe that there are unauthorized inquiries appearing on your credit report, you must challenge, in writing, whether or not the inquiring creditor had proper authorization to obtain your credit file. You should send letters to each inquiring creditor asking them to remove their inquiry.

20) Letter To Creditor Explaining Intention To File Bankruptcy

As noted in an earlier chapter of this book, bankruptcy is generally considered the last resort in debt management strategy. If you do decide that bankruptcy is your best alternative, you should notify all of your creditors in writing of your intentions. The letter should include your name, address, and the number of the account that will be included as debt in the bankruptcy proceedings.

21) Credit Information Dispute Form
Letter Requesting Credit Report

______________________________ (Today's Date)

________________________________ (Name of Credit Reporting Agency)

________________________________ (Mailing Address of CRA)

________________________________ (City, State and Zip Code)

Attention: Consumer Relations,

Please send me a copy of my credit report. I have enclosed a copy of my driver's license and a check (or money order) to cover the fee for a copy of my report.

My full name is: ____

My Social Security number is: ____________________________________

My date of birth is: ____

My home phone number is: ______________________________________

My current employer is: ____

My current address is: ____

____

____

Previous Address(s) (last five years):

____

____

Please forward my report to me at the above address.

Sincerely,

==

Letter Disputing Credit Report

____(date)

(your name and address)

____

____

__________________________(name and address of CRA)

____

____

Re: Dispute of Credit Report

To Whom It May Concern,

Please review the following inaccurate item(s) listed on my credit report. The items I dispute also are encircled on the attached copy of the report I received from your company.

1) ____

This item is inaccurate because

____

____

2) ____

This item is inaccurate because

____

3) ____

This item is inaccurate because ____________________

____

I am requesting that the item (s) be deleted or completed to correct the information on my report.

Please reinvestigate these disputed items and make the necessary corrections as soon as possible.

Sincerely,

Your Name and signature

Followup Letter Requesting Reinvestigation

______________________________ (date)

______________________________ (your name and address)
____
____

______________________________(name and address of CRA)

____

____

RE: Dispute Letter of ________________ (date of first dispute letter)

To whom it may concern,

On ________________ I sent you a written request for reinvestigation of inaccurate items on my credit report I received from your agency (I have enclosed a copy of the original letter I sent you with the disputed items encircled.).

Thirty days have passed and I have not received any response from you regarding this matter. Under the Fair Credit Reporting Act, you are required to respond within a "reasonable amount of time", typically 30 days.

Please notify me of the status of my request for reinvestigation as soon as possible.

Sincerely,

Letter Disputing Reinvestigation Findings

____________________________ (date)

____________________________________ (your name and address)

____

____

____________________________ (name and address of CRA)

____

____

RE: Dispute Investigation Findings

To whom it may concern,

I disagree with the findings of your investigation concerning the following disputed items:

____

____

____

Please re-investigate and provide me with the company names and addresses of those merchants with whom you verified the information so that I may contact them myself. Also advise me of your re-investigation findings and send me an updated copy of my credit report.

Sincerely,

Notice of Intent To File Formal Federal Trade Commission Complaint

_______________________ (date)

_______________________ (your name and address)
____
____

_______________________(name and address of CRA)
____
____

RE: Intent to File Formal FTC Complaint

To Whom It May Concern:

I am writing this letter to serve as a formal notice of my intent to file a complaint with the Federal Trade Commission, due to your failure to respond to my two previous letters requesting a reinvestigation of, and a correction to my credit report on file with your agency.

As shown by the enclosed copies of letters and postal receipts, your agency has received, by registered mail, a dispute letter dated __________, as well as a follow-up letter, dated ____________.

As you know, the Fair Credit Reporting Act requires you to respond to consumers' credit report disputes within 30 days, and that the FTC also investigates complaints for failure to respond. And yet, you have to this date, failed to respond.

I have advised you on two separate occasions, of the items I dispute in my credit report. I now advise you that if you do not immediately remove the inaccurate and incomplete information, I will file a formal complaint with the FTC. In addition, I also intend to seek redress in civil court to for recovery of damages, costs, and all attorney's fees, should you fail to respond.

I also expect you to provide me with a copy of my corrected credit report. Furthermore I expect you to provide a copy of my corrected report to all creditors who have received a copy of the incorrect report within the last six months, and the name, addresses, and telephone number of each credit grantor or other subscriber.

If your reinvestigation was negative, please notify me with a description of the procedure used to determine the accuracy and completeness of the information in my report to the above address.

Sincerely,

==

Formal Complaint Letter To The Federal Trade Commission

______________________ (date)

________________________ (your name and address)

____

____

Federal Trade Commission
Bureau of Credit Practices
Washington, DC 20580

To Whom It May Concern:

RE: Complaint ________________ (name of company)

I am writing this letter to file a formal complaint about

____

____

__________________________ (name and address of company).

My complaint regarding this company is as follows:

____

____

____

____

____

____

____

I understand that the FTC doesn't take action on behalf of individual consumers, however, I am writing you to make you aware of the problems I have been experiencing with ____________________. If you receive enough complaints about this company, I understand that you may take appropriate action to ensure that the company cannot continue to cause the same types of problems with other consumers.

Sincerely,

Your Name
and signature

Letter Requesting Addition of Accounts

________________________________ (date)

________________________________(your name and address)

____

____

________________________________(name and address of CRA)

____

RE: Addition of accounts

To whom it may concern,

Upon receipt of my credit report from your agency (your report or file number ___________), I have discovered that not all of my open accounts appear on the report. These unlisted accounts demonstrate prompt and timely payment histories and I would appreciate it if you would add them to my credit report. Listed below are the names of the creditors, their address and my account numbers with each creditor. I also have attached copies of my most recent statements from these accounts so you may verify their accuracy.

Creditor	Address	Account #
______________	______________	______________
______________	______________	______________

Please notify me when this information has been added to my credit report.

Sincerely,

Letter Requesting Inclusion of 100 Word Statement

_________________________ (date)

(your name and address)

____

____

____

_________________________ (name and address of CRA)

____

____

RE: Inclusion of 100 Word Statement To Credit Report

To whom it may concern,

Please include the following 100 word statement on my credit report on file with your agency (your file or credit report # _________________________).

____

____

____

____

____

____

____

Sincerely,

Letter Requesting Separate Credit Report

_____________________________ (date)

(your name and address)

____

____

____

_____________________________ (name and address of CRA)

____

____

RE: Removing spouse's name from credit report

To whom it may concern,

My credit report, which is on file with your agency, contains information about my spouse, as well as about me. I would appreciate it if you would remove my spouse's information from my report.

My Social Security number: _____________________________

Number of my file or report: _____________________________

My spouse's name: _____________________________

My spouse's Social Security number: _____________________________

Sincerely,

Letter Requesting Merger Of Spouse's Credit Report

_______________ (date)

(your name and address)

____

____

____

_______________ (name and address of CRA)

____

____

RE: Merger of spouse's credit report

To Whom It May Concern:

Please merge my credit report with that of my spouse. Please forward my updated file, as well as that of my spouse. I have enclosed copies of identification for both myself and my spouse.

My Social Security Number: _______________

My spouse's name: _______________

My spouse's Social Security number: _______________

Sincerely

Letter To Original Creditor Regarding Dispute Of Credit Report

_________________________ (date)

(your name and address)

____

____

____

________________________________ (name and address of CRA)

____

____

RE: Incorrect Credit Report

To Whom It May Concern:

My credit report from (name of CRA _________________________) contains the following incorrect entry: ____

____

____

Since the information is incorrect, I have asked that the entry be removed (corrected). However the credit reporting agency has informed me that you have verified incorrect information as a fact.

Below, as shown in the attached support documentation, is the correct information, which should be entered into my credit file.

____

____

I am requesting that you immediately contact this credit reporting agency and verify the correct information regarding my account with you. Please provide me with a copy of correspondence correcting this information. I am prepared to exercise my rights under the Fair Credit Reporting Act if you do not report and verify the correct information to this agency. I will expect a confirmation from you that the requested action has been taken, within three weeks.

Sincerely,

Letter To Creditor Disputing A Billing Error

________________________ (date)

(your name and address)

____

____

____

_______________________________ (name and address of CRA)

____

____

RE: Billing Error/Account # _______________________

To Whom It May Concern:

I am writing to dispute a billing error in the amount of $__________ on my account. The amount is inaccurate because

____

____

____

I am requesting that the error be corrected, that any finance and other charges related to the disputed amount be credited as well, and that I receive an accurate statement.

Enclosed are copies of supporting documents and information that will verify the accuracy of my claim. Please investigate this matter and correct the billing error as soon as possible.

Sincerely,
Enclosures: ____

Letter Closing An Account With A Creditor

________________________ (date)

(your name and address)

____

____

____

______________________________ (name and address of CRA)

____

____

RE: Closing My Account

To Whom It May Concern:

Please close my account number _____________________ with your company. I will no longer be using this account.

Sincerely,

Letter To A Creditor Requesting A Revised Payment Plan

________________________ (date)

(your name and address)

____

____

____

______________________________ (name and address of CRA)

____

____

RE: New Payment Plan

To Whom It May Concern:

My account number with your company is ________________. I recently have been experiencing some financial troubles and have been having difficulty paying on this account. While I intend to pay you the full amount due, I must confess that right now my financial situation leaves me incapable of making the originally agreed upon payments for this account. Therefore, I would like to arrange a payment plan as follows:

____

____

____

I also propose that as part of this plan, you will report my account to credit reporting agencies as follows:

____

____

____

Furthermore, I request that you respond to this proposal in writing within two weeks.
Sincerely,

Letter Requesting to Opt Out

_________________________ (date)

(your name and address)

____

____

____

______________________________ (name and address of CRA or other opt out program

____

____

RE: Removing name from mailing list

To Whom It May Concern:

I am writing this letter to request that the following name please be removed from your mailing list: ____

I also request that my name and address not be released to any other person or entity. I
do not want to receive mailings or phone calls from companies soliciting my business.

Sincerely,

Notice To Put Name On "Do Not Call" List

(your name and address)
____

____

____

____
(name and address of list maintainer)
____

____

____

RE: Adding name to don not call list

To Whom It May Concern:

This letter is in response to the telemarketing phone call I received from your company on ___________________. As I told your representative (company representative's name:_____________________) on _______________, I do not wish to receive telemarketing phone calls from your company. Therefore, I am formally requesting that you immediately put my name on your company's "do not call" list.

Sincerely,

Creditor Harassment Complaint Letter

(your name and address)

____

____

____

____

(name and address of creditor)

____

____

RE: Complaint of harassment

To Whom It May Concern:

I am writing this letter to inform you that at this time I am not able to pay my account in full because

____

____

____

However, according to the Fair Debt Collection Practices Act, I am entitled to be treated with dignity and respect. By the following actions, the collection agency you have enlisted to address my account is in violation of the law:

____

____

____

I will forego legal action, under my FCRA rights, including a law suit in small claims court for punitive damages. In return, I expect your assurance, in writing, that you and your collection agency will immediately and permanently cease all efforts to collect this obligation. In addition you also should remove all negative in formation regarding this account in my credit report.

Your immediate response is expected.

Sincerely,

===

Letter To Request Cessation of All Contact From A Creditor

(your name and address)

____

____

____

____

(name and address of creditor)

____

____

RE: Cessation of contact

To Whom It May Concern:

I am writing this letter to request that the Cease And Desist in your efforts to collect on the following account _________________________. Exercising my rights under the Federal Credit Collection Practices Act (Sec. 1692c), this letter serves as my formal notice for you to cease communication with me except as allowed by law.

Sincerely,

Letter To Creditor Regarding Unauthorized Credit Inquiry

(your name and address)

____

____

____

____

(name and address of creditor)

____

____

RE: Unauthorized credit inquiry

To Whom It May Concern:

Upon receiving a copy of my credit report from (name of CRA ______________________________), I have discovered a credit inquiry by your company that I have not authorized. I am aware that you should not be allowed to put an inquiry on my credit report unless I have authorized the inclusion.

Please remove this inquiry from my credit file because it is harming my ability to obtain credit.

As I need your immediate response to this letter, it has been sent by certified mail. Please provide me with any documentation proving that you have had the unauthorized inquiry removed.

Sincerely,

Letter To Creditor Explaining Intention To File Bankruptcy

_________________________________ (date)

(your name and address)

____

____

____

____

(name and address of creditor)

____

____

RE: Intention to File Bankruptcy

To Whom It May Concern:

I am writing to inform you that I am about to file bankruptcy, and that I will be including my debt (account # ________________________) to you in the proceedings.

Sincerely,

Credit Information Dispute Form

Full name: Last_______________ First _________________Middle ________

Current Address____

Former Address____

Social Security #__________________________

Home Phone_____________________________

Date of Birth_____________________________

Work Phone_____________________________

Employer_______________________________

Spouse Name____________________________

Spouse Social Security #___________________

Account Information

Company Name_____________________________

Account #____________________________

__ Not my account __ Was never late __Account paid in full
__ Current status incorrect __ Other

Explanation____

____

Company Name___________________________ Account #_____________

__ Not my account __ Was never late __Account paid in full
__ Current status incorrect __ Other

Explanation____

Company Name____________________Account #_____________________

__ Not my account __ Was never late __Account paid in full
__ Current status incorrect __ Other

Explanation____

Company Name_____________________ Account #_____________________

__ Not my account __ Was never late __Account paid in full
__ Current status incorrect __ Other

Explanation____

Courthouse or Collection Agency accounts:

Courthouseor Collections agency_____________________________

Case number for courthouse records only_______________________

__ Not Mine (explain) __ Satisfied __ Released __ Dismissed

__ Discharged __ Collection was paid __ Other (explain)

Explanation____

Courthouse or Collections agency____

Case number for courthouse records only____________________________________

__ Not Mine (explain) __ Satisfied __ Released __ Dismissed

__ Discharged __ Collection was paid __ Other (explain)

Explanation____

____________I certify that all information above is true and factual.

Signature____date______

Chapter 9

Frequently Asked Questions About Credit Reports

The final chapter of our Instant Credit Repair Kit manual addresses some of the most common questions concerning credit reporting agencies and the importance of consumer credit reports. The credit concerns of consumers like you and millions of others in the United States and the answers to those concerns— mainly how to repair and maintain good credit — are the foundation of this book. So, what follows in this final chapter is a summary, in question and answer format, is a summary of your rights as a consumer under the law for obtaining your credit history from a credit bureau and the process of disputing any mistakes in your credit record. In short, everything you need to know to repair your credit.

Q: Why should I check my credit report?

A. It's one thing to have poor credit, but it's something else altogether to have errors on your credit report through no fault of your own. Unfortunately, the result is the same — unless you check your report and correct the errors.

Consider this: you are much more likely to pay a higher interest rate on your car and mortgage with questionable credit. In addition, insurance companies can turn you down or put you in a higher risk category with higher premiums if they consider you a bad credit risk. And if that's not incentive enough, more employers now run credit checks for potential job selection and/or promotions.

A more appropriate question is, "why don't you check your credit report?"

Q: What rights do I have about finding out what information is in my report?

A: All you have to do is ask for your report. Under the Fair Credit Reporting Act (FCRA), the CRA must tell you everything that's in your report, including medical information, and in most cases, the sources of the information. The CRA also must give you a list of everyone who has requested your report within the past year — two years for employment-related requests.

Q: How can I find the CRA that has my credit report?

A: You can contact the CRAs listed in the Yellow Pages under "credit" or "credit rating and reporting." Because more than one CRA may have a credit file on you, call each until you locate all the agencies maintaining your file. Generally, however, credit reports are available from the big three credit reporting agencies: Equifax, Experian, and TransUnion (see Chapter 2 for information on how to contact the big three CRAs).

All smaller credit bureaus get their information from one of the big three agencies, which do not exchange information with each other. That's why each of the big three may have different information depending upon who has reported to them and what was reported. In other words, what is on one report may not be on another. You need to get a copy of your credit report from all three national credit reporting agencies, and you can do so by writing a "request for credit report" letter and sending a copy to each CRA.

Q: How much does a copy of my credit report cost?

A: By law, you are entitled to a free copy of your credit report if a company takes adverse action against you, such as denying your application for credit, insurance or employment, and you request your report within 60 days of receiving the notice of action. The notice will give you the name, address, and phone number of the CRA. In addition, you're entitled to one free report a year if, (1) you're unemployed and plan to look for a job within 60 days, (2) you're on welfare, or (3) your report is inaccurate because of fraud. Otherwise, a CRA may charge you up to $9 for a copy of your report.

Q: What do the CRAs need when I request my report?

A: Each CRA will require you to submit your full name, address (for the last 5 years), phone number, Social Security number, spouse's name and SSN, and usually proof of address (utility bill, etc.). You'll also need to enclose a check or money order for the appropriate fee (if applicable).

Q: What can I do about inaccurate or incomplete information in my credit report?

A: Under the amended FCRA, both the credit reporting agency and the information provider have responsibilities for correcting inaccurate or incomplete information in your credit report. To protect all your rights under this law, contact both the CRA and the information provider.

First of all, you should contact the CRA and explain in writing what information you believe is inaccurate. By law, CRAs must reinvestigate the items in question — usually within 30 days - unless they deem your dispute "frivolous". They also must forward all relevant data you provide about the items you dispute to the information provider. After the information provider receives notice of a dispute from the CRA, it must investigate, review all relevant information provided by the CRA, and report the results to the CRA. If the information provider finds the disputed information to be inaccurate, it must notify all nationwide CRAs so that they can correct this information in your credit file.

Once the reinvestigation is complete, the CRA must provide you with written results and a free copy of your report if the dispute results in a change. If an item is changed or removed, the CRA cannot put the disputed information back into your credit report unless the information provider verifies its accuracy and completeness, and the CRA provides you with a written notice that includes the name, address, and phone number of the provider.
The next step in the process is to tell the creditor or other information provider in writing that you dispute an item or items. Many providers specify a specific address for disputes. Some providers also have credit report disputes available online. If the provider then reports the item to any CRA, it must include a notice of your dispute. In addition, if you are correct and the information is inaccurate, the information provider may not use it again.

Q: What happens if the CRA or the information provider won't correct the information I dispute?

A: No matter certain you are that the items in your credit report that you dispute are indeed inaccurate or incomplete, a reinvestigation may not convince the CRA. In that event, you should ask the CRA to include your statement of the dispute in your file and in future reports. If you request, the CRA also will provide your statement to anyone who received a copy of the old report in the recent past. Typically, there is a fee for this service.

If you tell the information provider that you dispute an item, a notice of your dispute must be included anytime the information provider reports the item to a CRA.

Q: Can my boss get a copy of my credit report?

A: Under the law, your employer can only get a copy of your credit report if you say it's okay. A CRA may not supply information about you to your employer, or to a prospective employer, without your consent.

Q: Can creditors, employers, or insurers get a report that contains medical information about me?

A: No, not without your approval.

Q: How long can a CRA report negative credit information?

A: Generally negative information can remain in your credit report for seven years. There are, however, certain exceptions:

* Information about criminal convictions may be reported without any time limitation.
* Bankruptcy information may be reported for 10 years.
* Information reported in response to an application for a job with a salary of more than $75,000 has no time limit.
* Information reported because of an application for more than $150,000 worth of credit or life insurance has no time limit.
* Information about a lawsuit or an unpaid judgment against you can be reported for seven years or until the statute of limitations runs out, whichever is longer.

Q: Who, besides myself, can get a copy of my report?

A: Only people with a legitimate business need, as recognized by the FCRA. For example, a company is allowed to get your report if you apply for credit, insurance, employment, or to rent an apartment.

Q: What are "investigative consumer reports"?

A: These reports are use in connection with insurance and employment applications are detailed reports that include information gained from interviews with your neighbors or acquaintances about your life-style, character, and reputation.

You'll be notified in writing when a company orders an investigative consumer report. The notice will explain your right to request certain information about the report from the company you applied to. If your application is rejected, you may get additional information from the CRA. However, the CRA is not required to reveal the sources of its information.

Q: Can I stop a CRA from putting my name on lists for unsolicited credit and insurance offers?

A: Creditors and insurers may use CRA file information as a basis for sending you unsolicited offers. By law, these offers must include a toll-free number for you to call if you want to remove your name and address from lists for two years. Completing a form that the CRA provides for this purpose will keep your name off the lists permanently.

Q: Do I have the right to sue for damages?

A: According to your rights granted under the FCRA, you may sue a CRA, a user or — in some cases — a provider of CRA data, in state or federal court for most violations of the law. If you win the suit, the defendant will have to pay damages and reimburse you for attorney fees as ordered by the court.

Q: Are there any other laws that protect my rights as a consumer?

A: The federal government ahs enacted several laws to protect consumers. These laws cover various aspects of credit. For example, if your credit application was denied, the Equal Opportunity Act requires creditors to specify why — if you ask. If you do ask, the creditor must tell whether you were denied because you have "no credit file" with a CRA or because the CRA says you have "delinquent obligations." The ECOA also requires creditors to consider additional information you might supply about your credit history. You may want to find out why the creditor denied your application before you contact the CRA.

Q: Where should I report violations of federal law?

A: While the Federal Trade Commission can't act as your attorney in private disputes, information about your experiences and questions is important in the enforcement of the Fair Credit Reporting Act. Send your questions or formal complaints to: Consumer Response Center - FCRA, Federal Trade Commission, Washington, DC 20580.

Special Report #1

The Fair Credit Reporting Act: Your Rights And How To Use Them

Whenever you apply for credit, be it a charge account, a personal loan, insurance, or a job, there's a file about you. This file contains information on where you work and live, how you pay your bills, and whether you've been sued, arrested, or filed for bankruptcy,

Companies that gather and sell this information are called Consumer Reporting Agencies (CRAs). The most common type of CRA is the credit bureau. The information CRAs sell about you to creditors, employers, insurers, and other businesses is called a consumer credit report.

The Fair Credit Reporting Act (FCRA), enforced by the Federal Trade Commission, is designed to promote accuracy, fairness and privacy of the information in the files of every "consumer reporting agency". The FCRA gives you specific rights as outlined below in this report. You may have additional rights under state law. You may contact a state or local con summer protection agency or a state attorney general to learn those rights.

Under the FCRA, your rights are as follows:

* You must be told if the information in your credit report has been used against you. Anyone who uses information from a CRA to take action against you - such as denying an application for credit, insurance, or employment - must tell

you, and give you the name, address, and phone number of the CRA that provided the consumer report.

* You have the right to find out what is in your file. If you ask, a CRA must give you the information in your file, and a list of everyone who has requested it recently. There is no charge for the report if a person has taken action against you because of information supplied by the CRA, if you request the report within 60 days of receiving notice of the action. You also are entitled to one free report every year upon request if you can certify that (1) you are out of work and plan to seek employment within 60 days, (2) you are on welfare, or (3) your report is inaccurate due to fraud. Otherwise, a CRA may charge you up to nine dollars.

* You can dispute inaccurate information with the CRA. If you notify a CRA that your credit report contains inaccurate information, the CRA must investigate the items (usually within 30 days) by presenting to its information source all relevant evidence you submit, unless your dispute is considered frivolous. The information source must review your evidence and report its findings to the CRA. The CRA must give you a written report of the investigation, and a copy of your report if the investigation results in any change. If the CRA's investigation does not resolve the dispute, you may add a brief statement (100 words) to your file. The CRA must normally include a summary of your statement in future reports. If an item is deleted or a dispute statement is filed, you may ask that anyone who has recently received your report be notified of the change.

* Inaccurate information must be corrected or deleted. A CRA must remove or correct inaccurate or unverified information from its files, usually within 30 days, after you dispute.

* You have the right to dispute inaccurate items with the source of the information. If you tell anyone, such as a creditor who reports to a CRA, that you dispute an item, they may not then report the information to a CRA without including a notice of your dispute. In addition, once you've notified the source of the error in writing, it may not continue to report the information if it is, in fact, an error.

* Outdated information may not be reported. In most cases, a CRA may not report negative information that is more than seven years old; ten years for bankruptcies.

* Access to your credit report is limited. A CRA may provide information about you only to people with a need recognized by the FCRA - usually to consider an application with a creditor, insurer, employer, landlord, or other business.

* A CRA may not give out information about you to your employer, or prospective employer, without your written consent. A CRA may not report medical information about you to creditors, insurers, or employers without your permission.

* You may choose to exclude your name from CRA lists for unsolicited credit and insurance offers.

* If a CRA, a user or (in some cases) a provider of CRA data, violates the FCRA, you may sue them in state or federal court.

You can find the CRA that has your credit report by checking the Yellow Pages under "credit" or "credit rating and reporting." The three main national CRAs are:

1) Equifax: 1-800-685-1111; www.equifax.com
2) Exprian: 1-888-397-3742: www.experian.com
3) TransUnion: 1-800-916-8800; www.transunion.com

The FCRA gives several different federal agencies authority to enforce the law, primarily the Federal Trade Commission, Consumer Response Center -FCRA, Washington, DC 20580; 1-202-326-3761.

Special Report # 2

The Pros And Cons Of Personal Bankruptcy

Nearly 1.3 million individuals filed for personal bankruptcy in 2002. That's a staggering number of people who chose what is generally considered the last resort in debt management. While bankruptcy can give people who cannot pay their bills a fresh start, it is much more than a way of putting an end to nagging creditors and harassing debt collectors. It is in fact, a serious step - one that should be made only if it is the best way to deal with financial problems.

There are two basic types of bankruptcy available to most individuals:

Chapter 13 or "reorganization" allows debtors to keep property which they might otherwise lose, such as a mortgaged house or car. Reorganization may allow debtors to pay off or cure a default over a period of three to five years, rather than surrender property.

Chapter 7 or "straight bankruptcy" involves liquidation of all assets that are not exempt in your state. The exempt property may include items such as work-related tools and basic household furnishings, among others. Some of your property may be sold by a court-appointed official or turned over to your creditors. You can file for Chapter 7 only once every six years.

Both types of bankruptcy provide exemptions that permit most individual debtors to keep most of their assets, although these "exemption" amounts vary greatly from state to state.

The Pros Of Personal Bankruptcy

* Relieves the uncertainty and stress caused by worrying about money and dealing with creditors.
* Once an order is made, a third part become responsible for the administration, decision making and payment process of the debts.
* Creditors are forced to recognize that they must accept less money than is owed.
* Once discharged, most debts are written off and creditors cannot pursue them
* May get rid of unsecured debts
* May stop foreclosures, repossessions, garnishments, utility shutoffs, and debt collection activities.

The Cons of Personal Bankruptcy

* While bankruptcy has lost much of its stigma, a bankruptcy filing will invariably damage your credit rating.
* Information regarding bankruptcy may remain on your credit report for up to 10 years.
* May have difficulty getting credit or may be offered credit at unfavorable terms.
* May have difficulty renting an apartment.
* Co-signers may be hurt financially as a result of your bankruptcy filing.
* You may lose any realizable assets of value.
* Can be very expensive. Bankruptcy must be filed in federal court, with a filing fee around $175. This fee does not include the fees of your bankruptcy lawyer.
* You must allow all your financial affairs to be scrutinized, and can face criminal charges if irregularities are found.
* Bankruptcy usually does not wipe out child support payments, alimony, fines, taxes, and some student loan obligations.
* Unless under Chapter 13 you have an acceptable plan to catch up on your debt, bankruptcy usually does not permit you to keep prop-

erty when the creditor has an unpaid mortgage or lien in it.

If you are considering bankruptcy, choosing a lawyer may be difficult. Some of the least reputable lawyers make easy money by handling hundreds of bankruptcy cases without adequately considering individual needs. Recommendations from those you know and trust, and from employee assistance programs, are generally the most reliable.

Some public-funded legal services programs handle bankruptcy without charging attorney fees. Or these programs may provide referrals to private bankruptcy lawyers. You should understand, however that the fees these lawyers charge may very widely.

Making The Right Decision

There are always two sides to every story. Filing for personal bankruptcy does have several disadvantages, although most may seem trivial compared to dealing with overwhelming debt on a daily basis. Before you file for bankruptcy you need to carefully consider every issue involved and then determine if bankruptcy is indeed the best alternative for you.

One problem you must overcome is misinformation. Well-meaning friends and relatives may offer free advice on bankruptcy, but you need to know the facts before you decide. For example, you will not get fired from your job if you file for bankruptcy. Also, it will not cause you to lose your Social Security or other government benefits. As a matter of fact, the law provides that the government cannot discriminate against you because you have filed for bankruptcy.

Finally, filing for bankruptcy will not completely ruin your credit. Although it will affect your credit to some degree for up to 10 years, millions of individuals have been given a fresh start and rebuilt their good credit ratings after filing for personal bankruptcy. At any rate, it's a decision that will have a profound effect on your financial future, and should not be made lightly.

Special Report # 3

Debt Consolidation: An Alternative To Bankruptcy

Over 1 million people and businesses file for bankruptcy each year in the United States. Bankruptcy can have a very negative impact on your future ability to get credit. This impact can last for many years even after you have established a better credit rating. You should only use bankruptcy as a last resort when everything else has failed.

Are you having trouble paying your bills? Are you getting dunning notices from creditors? Are your accounts being turned over to debt collectors? Are you worried about losing your home or your car? You may want to consider these options: realistic budgeting, credit counseling from a reputable organization, debt consolidation, or bankruptcy. How do you know which will work best for you? It depends on your level of debt, your level of discipline, and your prospects for the future.

Debit Consolidation is one method that may be able to help you avoid filing for bankruptcy. By taking the proper actions you can stave off financial difficulties and get your debts under control. You can do the debt consolidation process yourself or get the help of a professional. Most banks or savings and loans companies offer this service. There are also independent professionals who offer debt consolidation. Here are a summary of the steps you should take, before you arrive at debt consolidation.

Develop a Budget

First take control of your financial situation by doing a realistic assessment of how much money comes in and how much money you spend. Start by listing your income from all sources. Then, list your "fixed" expenses-those that are the same each month-such as your mortgage payments or your rent, car payments, or insurance premiums. Next, list the expenses that vary, such as entertainment, recreation, or clothing. Writing down all your expenses-even those that seem insignificant-is a helpful way to track you're spending patterns, identify the expenses that are necessary, and prioritize the rest. The goal is to make sure you can make ends meet on the basics: housing, food, health care, insurance, and education.

You can then take a close look at this expenses list and start eliminating those that are not necessary - such as entertainment and eating out in restaurants. By eliminating all unnecessary expenses you will have more to pay the expenses that cannot be eliminated such as, rent, mortgages, and so forth.

Credit Counseling

If you aren't disciplined enough to create a workable budget and stick to it, can't work out a repayment plan with your creditors, or can't keep track of mounting bills, consider contacting a credit counseling service. Your creditors may be willing to accept reduced payments if you enter into a debt repayment plan with a reputable organization. In these plans, you deposit money each month with the credit counseling service. Your deposits are used to pay your creditors according to a payment schedule developed by the counselor. As part of the repayment plan, you may have to agree not to apply for-or use-any additional credit while you're participating in the program.

A successful repayment plan requires you to make regular, timely payments, and could take 48 months or longer to complete. Ask the credit counseling service for an estimate of the time it will take you to complete the plan. Some credit counseling services charge little or nothing for managing the plan; others charge a monthly fee that could add up to a significant charge over time. Some credit counseling services are funded, in part, by contributions from creditors. So you may want to check with more than one agency.

While a debt repayment plan can eliminate much of the stress that comes from dealing with creditors and overdue bills, it does not mean you can forget about your debts. You still are responsible for paying any creditors whose debts are not included in the plan. You are responsible for reviewing monthly statements from your creditors to make sure your payments have been received. If your repayment plan depends on your creditors agreeing to lower or eliminate interest and finance charges, or waive late fees, you are responsible for making sure these concessions are reflected on your statements.

A debt repayment plan does not erase your negative credit history. Accurate information about your accounts can stay on your credit report for up to seven years. In addition, your creditors will continue to report information about accounts that are handled through a debt repayment plan. For example, creditors may report that an account is in financial counseling, that payments have been late or missed altogether, or that there are write-offs or other concessions. A demonstrated pattern of timely payments, however, will help you get credit in the future.

Debt Consolidation

You may be able to lower your cost of credit by consolidating your debt through a second mortgage or a home equity line of credit. Think carefully before taking this on. These loans require your home as collateral. If you can't make the payments-or if the payments are late-you could lose your home. The costs of these consolidation loans can add up. In addition to interest on the loan, you pay "points. Still, these loans may provide certain tax advantages that are not available with other kinds of credit.

Some companies also offer debt consolidation loans. These are based upon your current income and ability to pay. They work by paying off all or most of your loans and consolidating them into one loan. Often this will result in a lower overall repayment. But this comes at a cost; you will be paying a high interest rate over a longer period of time, which means more overall money being taken from you. But you have gained time to help get your finances fixed.
So, if you are feeling overwhelmed by your debts, a debt consolidation program may be a better alternative than bankruptcy, in easing your financial burden and giving you a fresh start. Some debt consolidation plans can reduce your minimum payments by as much as 50% by working out modified payment arrangements with your creditors.

Once you begin a debt consolidation program, you make just one relatively low payment per month instead of struggling to pay all your creditors. It could be your best option for bringing your debt to a more manageable level. However, you should avoid the scams that promise to wipe out your debt, give you a guaranteed loan, or offer you instant credit repair. Most of these are promising something that they cannot delivery. If it sounds too good to believe, then it probably is a scam! Instead stick with a reliable financial institution.
Debt consolidation can be a valuable method for dealing with your debts and helping you to maintain good credit. If you have a reasonable amount of money coming in, and can also reduce some unnecessary expenses, it may be the right solution for your problem.

Special Report #4

How To Prepare Yourself To Buy A New Home

Buying a new home is one of the biggest financial decisions that you can make. You may still be able to purchase a home even if you have financial problems and a poor credit rating. There are a number of ways to get this accomplished.

If you have unpaid bills from the past and a poor credit rating you may not be able to get a loan from a bank or other regular financial institution. You should try to clean up your past overdue bills before using the alternate home financing methods described in this report. While this still won't result in a great credit rating it will provide evidence that you are a responsible person.

OWNER FINANCING

Sometimes a home seller will have trouble finding buyers who also qualify for a bank loan. In these cases the owner may offer to finance the home sale themselves. This type of arrangement is often known as a "land contract" It's a personal contract between the seller and the buyer. The agreement usually consists of a small down payment, a set amount of interest, monthly payments, and sometimes a damage deposit.

Usually the contract contains a default clause. If the buyer fails to make the agreed upon payments they lose the house and everything they have already paid into it, including the down payment and deposit. Therefore you must make certain that you are able to make the regular payments before you enter into this type of contract. It's a good idea to have an attorney look at the contract papers and you also should plan to have 2-3 months worth of the payments set aside for emergency purposes in case you lose your job.

FHA LOAN

The Federal Housing Administration (now under HUD) offers an alternate way to obtain home loans for first time buyers. By providing private lenders with mortgage insurance, the FHA gives them the security they need to lend to first-time buyers who might not be able to qualify for conventional loans. The FHA has helped more than 26 million Americans buy a home.

With the FHA, you don't need perfect credit or a high-paying job to qualify for a loan. The FHA also makes loans more accessible by requiring smaller down payments than conventional loans. In fact, an FHA down payment could be as little as a few months' rent. And your monthly payments may not be much more than rent.

There is no minimum income requirement. But you must prove steady income for at least three years, and demonstrate that you've consistently paid your bills on time. There are other requirements also such as: the amount of your current debt and the overall loan amount. You would need to be able to provide your current financial situation for the loan application papers.
Contact any lender such as a participating mortgage company, bank, savings and loan association, or thrift. Or visit the HUD web site at http://www.hud.gov or call a HUD-approved counseling agency at 1-800-569-4287 or TDD: 1-800-877-8339.

HUD LOANS

HUD, the U.S. Department of Housing and Urban Development was established in 1965 to develop programs to address housing needs in the U.S. HUD helps people by administering a variety of programs that develop and support affordable housing. HUD makes loans available for lower and moderate income families through its FHA mortgage insurance program and its HUD Homes program. HUD owns homes in many communities throughout the U.S. and offers them for sale at attractive prices and economical terms.
If you're buying a HUD Home, you're required to use a real estate agent. While purchasing a HUD Home may be easier than many private real estate transactions, there are still some requirements which must be met, certain forms that must be used, and procedures that must be followed. The initial listing price of each property is HUD's estimate of current fair market value and is based upon an appraisal conducted by an independent real estate appraiser.

HUD may accept an offer that's less than the listing price, depending on market conditions and the length of time the property has been on the market. Visit the web site at http://www.hud.gov or look in the phone book "blue pages" for a listing of the HUD office near you.

The listings above are the main alternate financing methods that are used to buy homes. However here are lesser known methods that can also be effective.

VA Loans are available for veterans. These loans are guaranteed by the Department of Veterans Affairs against loss to the lender, and made through a private lender. (HUD Homes may be purchased with a VA loan.)
Some home sellers will also agree to let you assume their current loan. You will need to get the approval of the loan institution for this method. This usually means that you will need no large down payment.

Fixer upper homes can often be had for a very low price depending upon what kind of shape they are in. You will need to examine these homes carefully and determine how much it will cost to repair the home.

Other methods include: Getting a home at a Sheriff's auction, usually for 2/3 of the appraised value. Or buying a property directly from the loan company. Sometimes you can obtain a great bargain on these types of homes.

If your credit rating is poor you can often use one of the above methods to purchase a home. And maybe save a lot of money in the process!

Special Report # 5

How To Get A Secured Credit Card

Many people have trouble getting a credit card due to their poor credit record. This problem can be solved by obtaining a secured credit card. Many financial institutions offer these special cards. However not all secured credit cards are equal. This report provides you with a list of factors to consider and a list of places where you can obtain secured credit cards.

Secured vs. Unsecured Cards

Secured and unsecured cards can be used to pay for goods and services. However, a secured card requires you to open and maintain a savings account as security for your line of credit; an unsecured card does not.

The required savings deposit for a secured card may range from a few hundred to several thousand dollars. Your credit line is a percentage of your deposit, typically 50 to 100 percent. Usually, a bank will pay interest on your deposit. In addition, you also may have to pay application and processing fees — sometimes totaling hundreds of dollars. Before you apply, be sure to ask what the total fees are and whether they will be refunded if you're denied a card. Typically, a secured card requires an annual fee and has a higher interest rate than an unsecured card. So you will want to compare interest rates and other special charges.

If you're considering a secured card as a way to build or re-establish a credit record, make sure the issuer reports to a credit bureau. Your credit history is maintained by companies called credit bureaus; they collect information reported to them by banks, mortgage companies, department stores, and other creditors. If your card issuer doesn't report to a bureau, the card won't help you build a credit history.

Shop around for the deal which is the best for your personal finances. Capital One and Cross Country are two banks currently with the easiest guidelines. Remember, the lenient secured credit cards are the most expensive. Here is a list of sources. Financial institutions sometimes change their policies - some of these companies may have changed their secured card services by the time you read this report. Some may have reached their "quotas" or dropped this service; therefore you may need to contact several banks. You should only apply at one bank at a time.

Amalgamated Bank of Chicago: MasterCard (800) 723-0300
American Pacific Bank Aumsville, OR : Visa (800) 610-1201
American Pacific Bank, Portland, OR: 800-879-8745
Bank One Tempe, AZ MasterCard/Visa
Cross Country Bank New Castle, DE: Visa/MasterCard (302) 322-3210 (800) 544-4110
Capital One Richmond, VA Visa/MasterCard : (888) 270-4298
Capital One Bridgeport, Ct: 800-333-7116
Citibank, the Lakes New York: 800-285-3000
Marine Midland, Buffalo NY : 800-874-2100
Sterling Bank & Trust Southfield, MI: MasterCard/Visa (800) 767-0923
AmeicOneCard Direct Deposit App. PO. Box 20847 Waco, Texas 76702-0847: 1- 254-741-9922
First National Bank Card Center, PO Box 98872, Las Vegas, NV 89193-8872: 1 (877) 825-3242
Bank One, Lafayette IN: 800395-2555
Spirit Visa, Parker CO: 800-779-8472
Commercial Bank of Detroit, Toledo OH: 800-841-0012
Ocean Independent Bank, Wilmington DE: 800-262-3610
Horizon B&T, Austin TX: 800-571-3462
First Western Bank, New Castle P: 800-837-6669
Some banks also advertise on the Internet. Just do a search for secured credit cards, and then contact the most promising ads. You will also want to check out all the financial institutions in your local area.
Here is a reliable source for an additional list of secured credit cards; the BankCard Holders of America (BHA) provides a list of institutions offering secured cards. Send a check or money order for $4.00 to: "Secured Credit Card List", BHA Customer Service, 524 Branch Drive, Salem, VA 24153

IMPORTANT INFORMATION

Getting a secured credit card is not automatic for some applicants. The way you fill out your application can sometimes affect the decision. Here are a few answers that the bank may view in a negative manner.

1. Any falsified information.
2. No telephone number
3. No permanent address, or living at someone else's address
4. No job or a low paying part-time job.
5. You should have no delinquent accounts for at least the past 6 months.
6. Applicant should have lived at their current residences for at least 1 year.
7. A large number of address changes will be viewed negatively.
8. Not having a checking or savings account.
9. Write neatly - a sloppily filled out application will lessen you chances.
10. Frequent changes in employment.
11. Using a PO Box as an address.
12. Bankruptcies

Getting a secured credit card can be one way to help improve your credit rating. If you use the card and make all the payments on time, that will help your credit rating to improve. You may then be able to get a regular unsecured credit card.

Special Report # 6

How To Rebuild Your Credit In The Shortest Time Possible

Once your credit rating has gone bad it will take some time to get it improved enough so that you will have no trouble getting new credit. Until then you may find it difficult or impossible to obtain a car loan, house loan, or any other type of major loan. There are many steps that you can take to improve your credit rating. The tips provided in this report will help you to repair your credit in the shortest time possible.

Step Number One

Your first step is to get rid of the current debts you have. That's right, before you can regain a good credit rating you need to pay off your debts. As long as you have old unpaid bills on your record you'll find it impossible to get new credit. You can do this by using several methods.

You should cut your expenses to the bare minimum and use the extra cash to catch-up on old bills. You may want to visit a debt consolidation expert and get a debt consolidation loan to repay old bills. You may be able to renegotiate and pay a smaller amount to settle an old debt that the creditor has written off.

Step Number Two

Get a copy of your credit report and look for any errors or inaccuracies. If you find errors you can dispute these with the credit agency and get them corrected. Also once you pay off old bills try to get the creditor to report that fact to the credit bureau. Request that they send a positive remark to add to your file. Examples: Paid as Agreed, Current Account (with no late payment), or Paid Satisfactory.

Making a Fresh Start

A bad Credit rating or bankruptcy will tarnish your credit report, but it is still possible to gain renewed confidence from creditors. You can typically obtain credit if you demonstrate a consistent employment record and signs of financial rehabilitation. Start by opening a savings account and obtaining a secured credit card. Make the payments on time to build a positive credit profile.

During your rebuilding period, it is important to check your credit rating often to make sure you are getting credit for your good deeds. Credit bureaus are required to provide a free copy of your credit report if you are denied credit. Some credit bureaus also provide a free copy once a year.

If you do not have a credit history, you should begin to build one. If you have a steady income and have lived in the same area for at least a year, try applying for credit with a local business, such as a department store. Or you might borrow a small amount from your credit union or the bank where you have checking and savings accounts. A local bank or department store may approve your credit application even if you do not meet the standards of larger creditors. Before you apply for credit, ask whether the creditor reports credit history information to credit bureaus serving your area. Most creditors do, but some do not. If possible, you should try to get credit that will be reported. This builds your credit history.

Another way to obtain credit is to get a co-signer for a loan that you might need. A co-signer is a person who pledges to pay the loan if you default on it. Once you get the loan make certain that you pay every installment on time. Your credit rating should improve once you have successfully paid off the loan.

A Final Word Of Advice

There are many people who advertise that they can repair your credit within a few weeks. Their advertisements make it sound like it is easy to regain your good credit rating by using their quick services. But you should avoid the services that promise you an easy way to good credit, most of them are scams. The best person to repair your credit is YOU!

You can quickly rebuild a good credit rating by dealing with your old debts, working out a responsible no frills budget, get a secured loan or credit card, and making your payments on time.

If you need help in dealing with your debts, you may want to contact a Consumer Credit Counseling Service (CCCS). This is a non-profit organization with more than 850 offices located in 50 states. CCCS counselors will try to arrange a repayment plan that is acceptable to you and your creditors. They will also help you set up a realistic budget and plan future expenses. You can find the CCCS office nearest you by checking the White Pages of your telephone directory or by calling from a touch-tone phone 1-800-388-2227 to get the telephone number

Special Report # 7

How To Stop Annoying Phone Calls From Creditors

If you use credit cards, owe money on a personal loan, or are paying on a home mortgage, you are officially a "debtor". Well, join the crowd. Most, if not all American consumers, are in debt to varying degrees. The problem is if you fall behind in repaying your creditors, or if an error is made on your accounts, you may be contacted by a "debt collector."

If you are in debt and are behind on paying your bills you have probably received a few (or many) phone calls from irate creditors. Nothing can be more annoying than getting an unfriendly phone call from a creditor when you are trying to relax at home. Can you stop these annoying calls? The answer is yes.

First let's consider a few facts. The first fact is that you are not a victim. If you have purchased items on credit you are obligated to repay the debt. If some-one owed you money you would probably contact them if they had not paid. So you should not try to cheat a creditor. You want to maintain a good credit rating for future purchases.

The second major fact is that not only do creditors have rights, but debtors also have rights. These rights protect you from harassment and other illegal debt collection practices. The debtor's rights have been enacted into law in the Fair Debt Collection Act (FDCA). This act details collection methods and practices that are illegal. If you know your legal rights you can stop illegal collection experts in their tracks.

Here are your rights under the Fair Debt Collection Act

1) Creditors cannot call you at your place of employment if your employer does not permit it (and most don't). This prevents them from harassing you at work and getting you in trouble with the boss.

2) Creditors may only call you at home between the hours of 8 am until 9 pm unless you agree otherwise.

3) They may not call you more than twice per week.

4) They may not make the debtor incur costs for communicating with them (no collect or long distance calls).

5) They cannot use threatening or abusive language in their communications.

6) You have the right to request that the creditor stop contacting you. Once you have made this request the creditor may only notify you one last time. They must either take legal action or forget the debt.

7) Within five days after you are first contacted, the collector must send you a written notice telling you the amount of money you owe, the name of the creditor to whom you owe the money; and what action to take if you believe you do not owe the money.

In addition, under the FDCA, debt collectors may not harass, oppress, or abuse anyone or any third parties they contact. For example, debt collectors may not:

* use threats of violence or harm
* publish a list of consumers who refuse to pay their debts (except to a credit bureau).
* Use obscene or profane language; or
* Repeatedly use the telephone to annoy someone;

Debt collectors also may not use any false statements when collecting a debt. For example, debt collectors may not:

* falsely imply that they are attorneys or government representatives;

* falsely imply that you have committed a crime;
* falsely represent that they operate or work for a credit bureau;
* misrepresent the amount of debt you owe;
* indicate that papers being sent to you are legal forms when they are not; or
* indicate that papers being sent to you are not legal forms when they are.

How may a debt collector contact you?

A collector may contact you in person, by mail, telegram, fax, or by telephone. However, a debt collector may not contact you at inconvenient times or places, such as before 8 a.m. or after 9 p.m. unless you agree.

How to stop a debt collector from contacting you

You can stop a debt collector from contacting you by writing a letter to the collection agency telling them to cease all further communication with you. Once the agency receives your letter, they may not contact you again except to inform you that there will be no further contact or to notify you that the debt collector or creditor intends to take some specific action. You should understand, however, that sending such a letter to a collector does not make your debt go away if you actually owe it. And you still could be sued by the debt collector or your original creditor.

What you can do if a debt collector violates the Fair Debt Collection Act

You have the right to sue a debt collector in a state or federal court within one year from the date the law was violated. If you win, you may recover money for any damages you suffered plus an additional amount up to $1,000. Court costs and attorney's fees also may be recovered.

Report any problems you have with a debt collector to your state Attorney Generals office, and the Federal Trade Commission. Many states have their own debt collection laws, and your Attorney Generals office can help you determine your rights.

To file a complaint with the FTC,
call toll-free 1-877-FTC-HELP (877-382-4357),
or visit the Web site at www.ftc.gov.

THE FAIR CREDIT REPORTING ACT

THE FAIR CREDIT REPORTING ACT

As a public service, the staff of the Federal Trade Commission (FTC) has prepared the following complete text of the Fair Credit Reporting Act (FCRA), 15 U.S.C. ß 1681 et seq. Although staff generally followed the format of the U.S. Code as published by the Government Printing Office, the format of this text does differ in minor ways from the Code (and from West's U.S. Code Annotated). For example, this version uses FCRA section numbers (ßß 601-625) in the headings. (The relevant U.S. Code citation is included with each section heading and each reference to the FCRA in the text.)
This version of the FCRA is complete as of January 7, 2002. It includes the amendments to the FCRA set forth in the Consumer Credit Reporting Reform Act of 1996 (Public Law 104-208, the Omnibus Consolidated Appropriations Act for Fiscal Year 1997, Title II, Subtitle D, Chapter 1), Section 311 of the Intelligence Authorization for Fiscal Year 1998 (Public Law 105-107), the Consumer Reporting Employment Clarification Act of 1998 (Public Law 105-347), Section 506 of the Gramm-Leach-Bliley Act (Public Law 106-102), and Sections 358(g) and 505(c) of the Uniting and Strengthening America by Providing Appropriate Tools Required to Intercept and Obstruct Terrorism Act of 2001 (USA PATRIOT Act) (Public Law 107-56).

TABLE OF CONTENTS

ß 603 Definitions; rules of construction
ß 604 Permissible purposes of consumer reports
ß 605 Requirements relating to information contained in consumer reports
ß 606 Disclosure of investigative consumer reports
ß 607 Compliance procedures
ß 608 Disclosures to governmental agencies
ß 609 Disclosures to consumers
ß 610 Conditions and form of disclosure to consumers
ß 611 Procedure in case of disputed accuracy
ß 612 Charges for certain disclosures
ß 613 Public record information for employment purposes
ß 614 Restrictions on investigative consumer reports
ß 615 Requirements on users of consumer reports
ß 616 Civil liability for willful noncompliance
ß 617 Civil liability for negligent noncompliance
ß 618 Jurisdiction of courts; limitation of actions
ß 619 Obtaining information under false pretenses
ß 620 Unauthorized disclosures by officers or employees
ß 621 Administrative enforcement
ß 622 Information on overdue child support obligations
ß 623 Responsibilities of furnishers of information to consumer reporting agencies
ß 624 Relation to State laws
ß 625 Disclosures to FBI for counterintelligence purposes
ß 626 Disclosures to governmental agencies for counterterrorism purposes
ß 601. Short title
This title may be cited as the Fair Credit Reporting Act.
ß 602. Congressional findings and statement of purpose [15 U.S.C. ß 1681]
(a) Accuracy and fairness of credit reporting. The Congress makes the following findings:
(1) The banking system is dependent upon fair and accurate credit reporting. Inaccurate credit reports directly impair the efficiency of the banking system, and unfair credit reporting methods undermine the public confidence which is essential to the continued functioning of the banking system.

(2) An elaborate mechanism has been developed for investigating and evaluating the credit worthiness, credit standing, credit capacity, character, and general reputation of consumers.
(3) Consumer reporting agencies have assumed a vital role in assembling and evaluating consumer credit and other information on consumers.

(4) There is a need to insure that consumer reporting agencies exercise their grave responsibilities with fairness, impartiality, and a respect for the consumer's right to privacy.

(b) Reasonable procedures. It is the purpose of this title to require that consumer reporting agencies adopt reasonable procedures for meeting the needs of commerce for consumer credit, personnel, insurance, and other information in a manner which is fair and equitable to the consumer, with regard to the confidentiality, accuracy, relevancy, and proper utilization of such information in accordance with the requirements of this title.

ß 603. Definitions; rules of construction [15 U.S.C. ß 1681a]

(a) Definitions and rules of construction set forth in this section are applicable for the purposes of this title.

(b) The term "person" means any individual, partnership, corporation, trust, estate, cooperative, association, government or governmental subdivision or agency, or other entity.

(c) The term "consumer" means an individual.

(d) Consumer report.

(1) In general. The term "consumer report" means any written, oral, or other communication of any information by a consumer reporting agency bearing on a consumer's credit worthiness, credit standing, credit capacity, character, general reputation, personal characteristics, or mode of living which is used or expected to be used or collected in whole or in part for the purpose of serving as a factor in establishing the consumer's eligibility for

(A) credit or insurance to be used primarily for personal, family, or household purposes;

(B) employment purposes; or

(C) any other purpose authorized under section 604 [ß 1681b].

(2) Exclusions. The term "consumer report" does not include

(A) any

(i) report containing information solely as to transactions or experiences between the consumer and the person making the report;

(ii) communication of that information among persons related by common ownership or affiliated by corporate control; or

(iii) communication of other information among persons related by common ownership or affiliated by corporate control, if it is clearly and conspicuously disclosed to the consumer that the information may be communicated among such persons and the consumer is given the opportunity, before the time that the information is initially communicated, to direct that such information not be communicated among such persons;

(B) any authorization or approval of a specific extension of credit directly or

indirectly by the issuer of a credit card or similar device;
(C) any report in which a person who has been requested by a third party to make a specific extension of credit directly or indirectly to a consumer conveys his or her decision with respect to such request, if the third party advises the consumer of the name and address of the person to whom the request was made, and such person makes the disclosures to the consumer required under section 615 [ß 1681m]; or
(D) a communication described in subsection (o).
(e) The term "investigative consumer report" means a consumer report or portion thereof in which information on a consumer's character, general reputation, personal characteristics, or mode of living is obtained through personal interviews with neighbors, friends, or associates of the consumer reported on or with others with whom he is acquainted or who may have knowledge concerning any such items of information. However, such information shall not include specific factual information on a consumer's credit record obtained directly from a creditor of the consumer or from a consumer reporting agency when such information was obtained directly from a creditor of the consumer or from the consumer.
(f) The term "consumer reporting agency" means any person which, for monetary fees, dues, or on a cooperative nonprofit basis, regularly engages in whole or in part in the practice of assembling or evaluating consumer credit information or other information on consumers for the purpose of furnishing consumer reports to third parties, and which uses any means or facility of interstate commerce for the purpose of preparing or furnishing consumer reports.
(g) The term "file," when used in connection with information on any consumer, means all of the information on that consumer recorded and retained by a consumer reporting agency regardless of how the information is stored.
(h) The term "employment purposes" when used in connection with a consumer report means a report used for the purpose of evaluating a consumer for employment, promotion, reassignment or retention as an employee.
(i) The term "medical information" means information or records obtained, with the consent of the individual to whom it relates, from licensed physicians or medical practitioners, hospitals, clinics, or other medical or medically related facilities.
(j) Definitions relating to child support obligations.
(1) Overdue support. The term "overdue support" has the meaning given to such term in section 666(e) of title 42 [Social Security Act, 42 U.S.C. ß 666(e)].
(2) State or local child support enforcement agency. The term "State or local child support enforcement agency" means a State or local agency which administers a State or local program for establishing and enforcing child sup-

port obligations.
(k) Adverse action.
(1) Actions included. The term "adverse action"
(A) has the same meaning as in section 701(d)(6) of the Equal Credit Opportunity Act; and
(B) means
(i) a denial or cancellation of, an increase in any charge for, or a reduction or other adverse or unfavorable change in the terms of coverage or amount of, any insurance, existing or applied for, in connection with the underwriting of insurance;
(ii) a denial of employment or any other decision for employment purposes that adversely affects any current or prospective employee;
(iii) a denial or cancellation of, an increase in any charge for, or any other adverse or unfavorable change in the terms of, any license or benefit described in section 604(a)(3)(D) [ß 1681b]; and
(iv) an action taken or determination that is
(I) made in connection with an application that was made by, or a transaction that was initiated by, any consumer, or in connection with a review of an account under section 604(a)(3)(F)(ii)[ß 1681b]; and
(II) adverse to the interests of the consumer.
(2) Applicable findings, decisions, commentary, and orders. For purposes of any determination of whether an action is an adverse action under paragraph (1)(A), all appropriate final findings, decisions, commentary, and orders issued under section 701(d)(6) of the Equal Credit Opportunity Act by the Board of Governors of the Federal Reserve System or any court shall apply.
(l) Firm offer of credit or insurance. The term "firm offer of credit or insurance" means any offer of credit or insurance to a consumer that will be honored if the consumer is determined, based on information in a consumer report on the consumer, to meet the specific criteria used to select the consumer for the offer, except that the offer may be further conditioned on one or more of the following:
(1) The consumer being determined, based on information in the consumer's application for the credit or insurance, to meet specific criteria bearing on credit worthiness or insurability, as applicable, that are established
(A) before selection of the consumer for the offer; and
(B) for the purpose of determining whether to extend credit or insurance pursuant to the offer.
(2) Verification
(A) that the consumer continues to meet the specific criteria used to select the consumer for the offer, by using information in a consumer report on the con-

sumer, information in the consumer's application for the credit or insurance, or other information bearing on the credit worthiness or insurability of the consumer; or

(B) of the information in the consumer's application for the credit or insurance, to determine that the consumer meets the specific criteria bearing on credit worthiness or insurability.

(3) The consumer furnishing any collateral that is a requirement for the extension of the credit or insurance that was

(A) established before selection of the consumer for the offer of credit or insurance; and

(B) disclosed to the consumer in the offer of credit or insurance.

(m) Credit or insurance transaction that is not initiated by the consumer. The term"credit or insurance transaction that is not initiated by the consumer" does not include the use of a consumer report by a person with which the consumer has an account or insurance policy, for purposes of

(1) reviewing the account or insurance policy; or

(2) collecting the account.

(n) State. The term "State" means any State, the Commonwealth of Puerto Rico, the District of Columbia, and any territory or possession of the United States.

(o) Excluded communications. A communication is described in this subsection if it is a communication

(1) that, but for subsection (d)(2)(D), would be an investigative consumer report;

(2) that is made to a prospective employer for the purpose of

(A) procuring an employee for the employer; or

(B) procuring an opportunity for a natural person to work for the employer;

(3) that is made by a person who regularly performs such procurement;

(4) that is not used by any person for any purpose other than a purpose described in subparagraph (A) or (B) of paragraph (2); and

(5) with respect to which

(A) the consumer who is the subject of the communication

(i) consents orally or in writing to the nature and scope of the communication, before the collection of any information for the purpose of making the communication;

(ii) consents orally or in writing to the making of the communication to a prospective employer, before the making of the communication; and

(iii) in the case of consent under clause (i) or (ii) given orally, is provided written confirmation of that consent by the person making the communication, not later than 3 business days after the receipt of the consent by that person;

(B) the person who makes the communication does not, for the purpose of making the communication, make any inquiry that if made by a prospective employer of the consumer who is the subject of the communication would violate any applicable Federal or State equal employment opportunity law or regulation; and
(C) the person who makes the communication
(i) discloses in writing to the consumer who is the subject of the communication, not later than 5 business days after receiving any request from the consumer for such disclosure, the nature and substance of all information in the consumer's file at the time of the request, except that the sources of any information that is acquired solely for use in making the communication and is actually used for no other purpose, need not be disclosed other than under appropriate discovery procedures in any court of competent jurisdiction in which an action is brought; and
(ii) notifies the consumer who is the subject of the communication, in writing, of the consumer's right to request the information described in clause (i).
(p) Consumer reporting agency that compiles and maintains files on consumers on a nationwide basis. The term "consumer reporting agency that compiles and maintains files on consumers on a nationwide basis" means a consumer reporting agency that regularly engages in the practice of assembling or evaluating, and maintaining, for the purpose of furnishing consumer reports to third parties bearing on a consumer's credit worthiness, credit standing, or credit capacity, each of the following regarding consumers residing nationwide:
(1) Public record information.
(2) Credit account information from persons who furnish that information regularly and in the ordinary course of business.
ß 604. Permissible purposes of consumer reports [15 U.S.C. ß 1681b]
(a) In general. Subject to subsection (c), any consumer reporting agency may furnish a consumer report under the following circumstances and no other:
(1) In response to the order of a court having jurisdiction to issue such an order, or a subpoena issued in connection with proceedings before a Federal grand jury.
(2) In accordance with the written instructions of the consumer to whom it relates.
(3) To a person which it has reason to believe
(A) intends to use the information in connection with a credit transaction involving the consumer on whom the information is to be furnished and involving the extension of credit to, or review or collection of an account of, the consumer; or

(B) intends to use the information for employment purposes; or
(C) intends to use the information in connection with the underwriting of insurance involving the consumer; or
(D) intends to use the information in connection with a determination of the consumer's eligibility for a license or other benefit granted by a governmental instrumentality required by law to consider an applicant's financial responsibility or status; or
(E) intends to use the information, as a potential investor or servicer, or current insurer, in connection with a valuation of, or an assessment of the credit or prepayment risks associated with, an existing credit obligation; or
(F) otherwise has a legitimate business need for the information
(i) in connection with a business transaction that is initiated by the consumer; or
(ii) to review an account to determine whether the consumer continues to meet the terms of the account.
(4) In response to a request by the head of a State or local child support enforcement agency (or a State or local government official authorized by the head of such an agency), if the person making the request certifies to the consumer reporting agency that
(A) the consumer report is needed for the purpose of establishing an individual's capacity to make child support payments or determining the appropriate level of such payments;
(B) the paternity of the consumer for the child to which the obligation relates has been established or acknowledged by the consumer in accordance with State laws under which the obligation arises (if required by those laws);
(C) the person has provided at least 10 days' prior notice to the consumer whose report is requested, by certified or registered mail to the last known address of the consumer, that the report will be requested; and
(D) the consumer report will be kept confidential, will be used solely for a purpose described in subparagraph (A), and will not be used in connection with any other civil, administrative, or criminal proceeding, or for any other purpose.
(5) To an agency administering a State plan under Section 454 of the Social Security Act (42 U.S.C. ß 654) for use to set an initial or modified child support award.
(b) Conditions for furnishing and using consumer reports for employment purposes.
(1) Certification from user. A consumer reporting agency may furnish a consumer report for employment purposes only if
(A) the person who obtains such report from the agency certifies to the agency that

(i) the person has complied with paragraph (2) with respect to the consumer report, and the person will comply with paragraph (3) with respect to the consumer report if paragraph (3) becomes applicable; and
(ii) information from the consumer report will not be used in violation of any applicable Federal or State equal employment opportunity law or regulation; and
(B) the consumer reporting agency provides with the report, or has previously provided, a summary of the consumer's rights under this title, as prescribed by the Federal Trade Commission under section 609(c)(3) [ß 1681g].
(2) Disclosure to consumer.
(A) In general. Except as provided in subparagraph (B), a person may not procure a consumer report, or cause a consumer report to be procured, for employment purposes with respect to any consumer, unless—
(i) a clear and conspicuous disclosure has been made in writing to the consumer at any time before the report is procured or caused to be procured, in a document that consists solely of the disclosure, that a consumer report may be obtained for employment purposes; and
(ii) the consumer has authorized in writing (which authorization may be made on the document referred to in clause (i)) the procurement of the report by that person.
(B) Application by mail, telephone, computer, or other similar means. If a consumer described in subparagraph (C) applies for employment by mail, telephone, computer, or other similar means, at any time before a consumer report is procured or caused to be procured in connection with that application—
(i) the person who procures the consumer report on the consumer for employment purposes shall provide to the consumer, by oral, written, or electronic means, notice that a consumer report may be obtained for employment purposes, and a summary of the consumer's rights under section 615(a)(3); and
(ii) the consumer shall have consented, orally, in writing, or electronically to the procurement of the report by that person.
(C) Scope. Subparagraph (B) shall apply to a person procuring a consumer report on a consumer in connection with the consumer's application for employment only if—

(i) the consumer is applying for a position over which the Secretary of Transportation has the power to establish qualifications and maximum hours of service pursuant to the provisions of section 31502 of title 49, or a position subject to safety regulation by a State transportation agency; and
(ii) as of the time at which the person procures the report or causes the report to be procured the only interaction between the consumer and the person in

connection with that employment application has been by mail, telephone, computer, or other similar means.

(3) Conditions on use for adverse actions.

(A) In general. Except as provided in subparagraph (B), in using a consumer report for employment purposes, before taking any adverse action based in whole or in part on the report, the person intending to take such adverse action shall provide to the consumer to whom the report relates—

(i) a copy of the report; and

(ii) a description in writing of the rights of the consumer under this title, as prescribed by the Federal Trade Commission under section 609(c)(3).

(B) Application by mail, telephone, computer, or other similar means.

(i) If a consumer described in subparagraph (C) applies for employment by mail, telephone, computer, or other similar means, and if a person who has procured a consumer report on the consumer for employment purposes takes adverse action on the employment application based in whole or in part on the report, then the person must provide to the consumer to whom the report relates, in lieu of the notices required under subparagraph (A) of this section and under section 615(a), within 3 business days of taking such action, an oral, written or electronic notification—

(I) that adverse action has been taken based in whole or in part on a consumer report received from a consumer reporting agency;

(II) of the name, address and telephone number of the consumer reporting agency that furnished the consumer report (including a toll-free telephone number established by the agency if the agency compiles and maintains files on consumers on a nationwide basis);

(III) that the consumer reporting agency did not make the decision to take the adverse action and is unable to provide to the consumer the specific reasons why the adverse action was taken; and

(IV) that the consumer may, upon providing proper identification, request a free copy of a report and may dispute with the consumer reporting agency the accuracy or completeness of any information in a report.

(ii) If, under clause (B)(i)(IV), the consumer requests a copy of a consumer report from the person who procured the report, then, within 3 business days of receiving the consumer's request, together with proper identification, the person must send or provide to the consumer a copy of a report and a copy of the consumer's rights as prescribed by the Federal Trade Commission under section 609(c)(3).

(C) Scope. Subparagraph (B) shall apply to a person procuring a consumer report on a consumer in connection with the consumer's application for employment only if—

(i) the consumer is applying for a position over which the Secretary of Transportation has the power to establish qualifications and maximum hours of service pursuant to the provisions of section 31502 of title 49, or a position subject to safety regulation by a State transportation agency; and

(ii) as of the time at which the person procures the report or causes the report to be procured the only interaction between the consumer and the person in connection with that employment application has been by mail, telephone, computer, or other similar means.

(4) Exception for national security investigations.

(A) In general. In the case of an agency or department of the United States Government which seeks to obtain and use a consumer report for employment purposes, paragraph (3) shall not apply to any adverse action by such agency or department which is based in part on such consumer report, if the head of such agency or department makes a written finding that—

(i) the consumer report is relevant to a national security investigation of such agency or department;

(ii) the investigation is within the jurisdiction of such agency or department;

(iii) there is reason to believe that compliance with paragraph (3) will—

(I) endanger the life or physical safety of any person;

(II) result in flight from prosecution;

(III) result in the destruction of, or tampering with, evidence relevant to the investigation;

(IV) result in the intimidation of a potential witness relevant to the investigation;

(V) result in the compromise of classified information; or

(VI) otherwise seriously jeopardize or unduly delay the investigation or another official proceeding.

(B) Notification of consumer upon conclusion of investigation. Upon the conclusion of a national security investigation described in subparagraph (A), or upon the determination that the exception under subparagraph (A) is no longer required for the reasons set forth in such subparagraph, the official exercising the authority in such subparagraph shall provide to the consumer who is the subject of the consumer report with regard to which such finding was made—

(i) a copy of such consumer report with any classified information redacted as necessary;

(ii) notice of any adverse action which is based, in part, on the consumer report; and

(iii) the identification with reasonable specificity of the nature of the investigation for which the consumer report was sought.

(C) Delegation by head of agency or department. For purposes of subparagraphs (A) and (B), the head of any agency or department of the United States

Government may delegate his or her authorities under this paragraph to an official of such agency or department who has personnel security responsibilities and is a member of the Senior Executive Service or equivalent civilian or military rank.

(D) Report to the congress. Not later than January 31 of each year, the head of each agency and department of the United States Government that exercised authority under this paragraph during the preceding year shall submit a report to the Congress on the number of times the department or agency exercised such authority during the year.

(E) Definitions. For purposes of this paragraph, the following definitions shall apply:

(i) Classified information. The term `classified information' means information that is protected from unauthorized disclosure under Executive Order No. 12958 or successor orders.

(ii) National security investigation. The term `national security investigation' means any official inquiry by an agency or department of the United States Government to determine the eligibility of a consumer to receive access or continued access to classified information or to determine whether classified information has been lost or compromised.

(c) Furnishing reports in connection with credit or insurance transactions that are not initiated by the consumer.

(1) In general. A consumer reporting agency may furnish a consumer report relating to any consumer pursuant to subparagraph (A) or (C) of subsection (a)(3) in connection with any credit or insurance transaction that is not initiated by the consumer only if

(A) the consumer authorizes the agency to provide such report to such person; or

(B) (i) the transaction consists of a firm offer of credit or insurance;

(ii) the consumer reporting agency has complied with subsection (e); and

(iii) there is not in effect an election by the consumer, made in accordance with subsection (e), to have the consumer's name and address excluded from lists of names provided by the agency pursuant to this paragraph.

(2) Limits on information received under paragraph (1)(B). A person may receive pursuant to paragraph (1)(B) only

(A) the name and address of a consumer;

(B) an identifier that is not unique to the consumer and that is used by the person solely for the purpose of verifying the identity of the consumer; and

(C) other information pertaining to a consumer that does not identify the relationship or experience of the consumer with respect to a particular creditor or other entity.

(3) Information regarding inquiries. Except as provided in section 609(a)(5) [ß 1681g], a consumer reporting agency shall not furnish to any person a record of inquiries in connection with a credit or insurance transaction that is not initiated by a consumer.
(d) Reserved.
(e) Election of consumer to be excluded from lists.
(1) In general. A consumer may elect to have the consumer's name and address excluded from any list provided by a consumer reporting agency under subsection (c)(1)(B) in connection with a credit or insurance transaction that is not initiated by the consumer, by notifying the agency in accordance with paragraph (2) that the consumer does not consent to any use of a consumer report relating to the consumer in connection with any credit or insurance transaction that is not initiated by the consumer.
(2) Manner of notification. A consumer shall notify a consumer reporting agency under paragraph (1)
(A) through the notification system maintained by the agency under paragraph (5); or
(B) by submitting to the agency a signed notice of election form issued by the agency for purposes of this subparagraph.
(3) Response of agency after notification through system. Upon receipt of notification of the election of a consumer under paragraph (1) through the notification system maintained by the agency under paragraph (5), a consumer reporting agency shall
(A) inform the consumer that the election is effective only for the 2-year period following the election if the consumer does not submit to the agency a signed notice of election form issued by the agency for purposes of paragraph (2)(B); and
(B) provide to the consumer a notice of election form, if requested by the consumer, not later than 5 business days after receipt of the notification of the election through the system established under paragraph (5), in the case of a request made at the time the consumer provides notification through the system.
(4) Effectiveness of election. An election of a consumer under paragraph (1)
(A) shall be effective with respect to a consumer reporting agency beginning 5 business days after the date on which the consumer notifies the agency in accordance with paragraph (2);
(B) shall be effective with respect to a consumer reporting agency
(i) subject to subparagraph (C), during the 2-year period beginning 5 business days after the date on which the consumer notifies the agency of the election, in the case of an election for which a consumer notifies the agency only in

accordance with paragraph (2)(A); or
(ii) until the consumer notifies the agency under subparagraph (C), in the case of an election for which a consumer notifies the agency in accordance with paragraph (2)(B);
(C) shall not be effective after the date on which the consumer notifies the agency, through the notification system established by the agency under paragraph (5), that the election is no longer effective; and
(D) shall be effective with respect to each affiliate of the agency.
(5) Notification system.
(A) In general. Each consumer reporting agency that, under subsection (c)(1)(B), furnishes a consumer report in connection with a credit or insurance transaction that is not initiated by a consumer, shall
(i) establish and maintain a notification system, including a toll-free telephone number, which permits any consumer whose consumer report is maintained by the agency to notify the agency, with appropriate identification, of the consumer's election to have the consumer's name and address excluded from any such list of names and addresses provided by the agency for such a transaction; and
(ii) publish by not later than 365 days after the date of enactment of the Consumer Credit Reporting Reform Act of 1996, and not less than annually thereafter, in a publication of general circulation in the area served by the agency
(I) a notification that information in consumer files maintained by the agency may be used in connection with such transactions; and
(II) the address and toll-free telephone number for consumers to use to notify the agency of the consumer's election under clause (I).
(B) Establishment and maintenance as compliance. Establishment and maintenance of a notification system (including a toll-free telephone number) and publication by a consumer reporting agency on the agency's own behalf and on behalf of any of its affiliates in accordance with this paragraph is deemed to be compliance with this paragraph by each of those affiliates.
(6) Notification system by agencies that operate nationwide. Each consumer reporting agency that compiles and maintains files on consumers on a nationwide basis shall establish and maintain a notification system for purposes of paragraph (5) jointly with other such consumer reporting agencies.
(f) Certain use or obtaining of information prohibited. A person shall not use or obtain a consumer report for any purpose unless
(1) the consumer report is obtained for a purpose for which the consumer report is authorized to be furnished under this section; and
(2) the purpose is certified in accordance with section 607 [ß 1681e] by a

prospective user of the report through a general or specific certification.

(g) Furnishing reports containing medical information. A consumer reporting agency shall not furnish for employment purposes, or in connection with a credit or insurance transaction, a consumer report that contains medical information about a consumer, unless the consumer consents to the furnishing of the report.

ß 605. Requirements relating to information contained in consumer reports [15 U.S.C. ß 1681c]

(a) Information excluded from consumer reports. Except as authorized under subsection (b) of this section, no consumer reporting agency may make any consumer report containing any of the following items of information:

(1) Cases under title 11 [United States Code] or under the Bankruptcy Act that, from the date of entry of the order for relief or the date of adjudication, as the case may be, antedate the report by more than 10 years.

(2) Civil suits, civil judgments, and records of arrest that from date of entry, antedate the report by more than seven years or until the governing statute of limitations has expired, whichever is the longer period.

(3) Paid tax liens which, from date of payment, antedate the report by more than seven years.

(4) Accounts placed for collection or charged to profit and loss which antedate the report by more than seven years.(1)

(5) Any other adverse item of information, other than records of convictions of crimes which antedates the report by more than seven years.1

(b) Exempted cases. The provisions of subsection (a) of this section are not applicable in the case of any consumer credit report to be used in connection with

(1) a credit transaction involving, or which may reasonably be expected to involve, a principal amount of $150,000 or more;

(2) the underwriting of life insurance involving, or which may reasonably be expected to involve, a face amount of $150,000 or more; or

(3) the employment of any individual at an annual salary which equals, or which may reasonably be expected to equal $75,000, or more.

(c) Running of reporting period.

(1) In general. The 7-year period referred to in paragraphs (4) and (6)(2) of subsection (a) shall begin, with respect to any delinquent account that is placed for collection (internally or by referral to a third party, whichever is earlier), charged to profit and loss, or subjected to any similar action, upon the expiration of the 180-day period beginning on the date of the commencement of the delinquency which immediately preceded the collection activity, charge to profit and loss, or similar action.

(2) Effective date. Paragraph (1) shall apply only to items of information added to the file of a consumer on or after the date that is 455 days after the date of enactment of the Consumer Credit Reporting Reform Act of 1996.
(d) Information required to be disclosed. Any consumer reporting agency that furnishes a consumer report that contains information regarding any case involving the consumer that arises under title 11, United States Code, shall include in the report an identification of the chapter of such title 11 under which such case arises if provided by the source of the information. If any case arising or filed under title 11, United States Code, is withdrawn by the consumer before a final judgment, the consumer reporting agency shall include in the report that such case or filing was withdrawn upon receipt of documentation certifying such withdrawal.
(e) Indication of closure of account by consumer. If a consumer reporting agency is notified pursuant to section 623(a)(4) [ß 1681s-2] that a credit account of a consumer was voluntarily closed by the consumer, the agency shall indicate that fact in any consumer report that includes information related to the account.
(f) Indication of dispute by consumer. If a consumer reporting agency is notified pursuant to section 623(a)(3) [ß 1681s-2] that information regarding a consumer who was furnished to the agency is disputed by the consumer, the agency shall indicate that fact in each consumer report that includes the disputed information.
ß 606. Disclosure of investigative consumer reports [15 U.S.C. ß 1681d]
(a) Disclosure of fact of preparation. A person may not procure or cause to be prepared an investigative consumer report on any consumer unless
(1) it is clearly and accurately disclosed to the consumer that an investigative consumer report including information as to his character, general reputation, personal characteristics and mode of living, whichever are applicable, may be made, and such disclosure
(A) is made in a writing mailed, or otherwise delivered, to the consumer, not later than three days after the date on which the report was first requested, and
(B) includes a statement informing the consumer of his right to request the additional disclosures provided for under subsection (b) of this section and the written summary of the rights of the consumer prepared pursuant to section 609(c) [ß 1681g]; and
(2) the person certifies or has certified to the consumer reporting agency that

(A) the person has made the disclosures to the consumer required by paragraph (1); and
(B) the person will comply with subsection (b).

(b) Disclosure on request of nature and scope of investigation. Any person who procures or causes to be prepared an investigative consumer report on any consumer shall, upon written request made by the consumer within a reasonable period of time after the receipt by him of the disclosure required by subsection (a)(1) of this section, make a complete and accurate disclosure of the nature and scope of the investigation requested. This disclosure shall be made in a writing mailed, or otherwise delivered, to the consumer not later than five days after the date on which the request for such disclosure was received from the consumer or such report was first requested, whichever is the later.

(c) Limitation on liability upon showing of reasonable procedures for compliance with provisions. No person may be held liable for any violation of subsection (a) or (b) of this section if he shows by a preponderance of the evidence that at the time of the violation he maintained reasonable procedures to assure compliance with subsection (a) or (b) of this section.

(d) Prohibitions.

(1) Certification. A consumer reporting agency shall not prepare or furnish investigative consumer report unless the agency has received a certification under subsection (a)(2) from the person who requested the report.

(2) Inquiries. A consumer reporting agency shall not make an inquiry for the purpose of preparing an investigative consumer report on a consumer for employment purposes if the making of the inquiry by an employer or prospective employer of the consumer would violate any applicable Federal or State equal employment opportunity law or regulation.

(3) Certain public record information. Except as otherwise provided in section 613 [ß 1681k], a consumer reporting agency shall not furnish an investigative consumer report that includes information that is a matter of public record and that relates to an arrest, indictment, conviction, civil judicial action, tax lien, or outstanding judgment, unless the agency has verified the accuracy of the information during the 30-day period ending on the date on which the report is furnished.

(4) Certain adverse information. A consumer reporting agency shall not prepare or furnish an investigative consumer report on a consumer that contains information that is adverse to the interest of the consumer and that is obtained through a personal interview with a neighbor, friend, or associate of the consumer or with another person with whom the consumer is acquainted or who has knowledge of such item of information, unless

(A) the agency has followed reasonable procedures to obtain confirmation of the information, from an additional source that has independent and direct knowledge of the information; or

(B) the person interviewed is the best possible source of the information.
ß 607. Compliance procedures [15 U.S.C. ß 1681e]
(a) Identity and purposes of credit users. Every consumer reporting agency shall maintain reasonable procedures designed to avoid violations of section 605 [ß 1681c] and to limit the furnishing of consumer reports to the purposes listed under section 604 [ß 1681b] of this title. These procedures shall require that prospective users of the information identify themselves, certify the purposes for which the information is sought, and certify that the information will be used for no other purpose. Every consumer reporting agency shall make a reasonable effort to verify the identity of a new prospective user and the uses certified by such prospective user prior to furnishing such user a consumer report. No consumer reporting agency may furnish a consumer report to any person if it has reasonable grounds for believing that the consumer report will not be used for a purpose listed in section 604 [ß 1681b] of this title.
(b) Accuracy of report. Whenever a consumer reporting agency prepares a consumer report it shall follow reasonable procedures to assure maximum possible accuracy of the information concerning the individual about whom the report relates.
(c) Disclosure of consumer reports by users allowed. A consumer reporting agency may not prohibit a user of a consumer report furnished by the agency on a consumer from disclosing the contents of the report to the consumer, if adverse action against the consumer has been taken by the user based in whole or in part on the report.
(d) Notice to users and furnishers of information.
(1) Notice requirement. A consumer reporting agency shall provide to any person
(A) who regularly and in the ordinary course of business furnishes information to the agency with respect to any consumer; or

(B) to whom a consumer report is provided by the agency;

a notice of such person's responsibilities under this title.

(2) Content of notice. The Federal Trade Commission shall prescribe the content of notices under paragraph (1), and a consumer reporting agency shall be in compliance with this subsection if it provides a notice under paragraph (1) that is substantially similar to the Federal Trade Commission prescription under this paragraph.
(e) Procurement of consumer report for resale.

(1) Disclosure. A person may not procure a consumer report for purposes of reselling the report (or any information in the report) unless the person discloses to the consumer reporting agency that originally furnishes the report
(A) the identity of the end-user of the report (or information); and
(B) each permissible purpose under section 604 [ß 1681b] for which the report is furnished to the end-user of the report (or information).
(2) Responsibilities of procurers for resale. A person who procures a consumer report for purposes of reselling the report (or any information in the report) shall

(A) establish and comply with reasonable procedures designed to ensure that the report (or information) is resold by the person only for a purpose for which the report may be furnished under section 604 [ß 1681b], including by requiring that each person to which the report (or information) is resold and that resells or provides the report (or information) to any other person
(i) identifies each end user of the resold report (or information);
(ii) certifies each purpose for which the report (or information) will be used; and
(iii) certifies that the report (or information) will be used for no other purpose; and

(B) before reselling the report, make reasonable efforts to verify the identifications and certifications made under subparagraph (A).
(3) Resale of consumer report to a federal agency or department. Notwithstanding paragraph (1) or (2), a person who procures a consumer report for purposes of reselling the report (or any information in the report) shall not disclose the identity of the end-user of the report under paragraph (1) or (2) if—

(A) the end user is an agency or department of the United States Government which procures the report from the person for purposes of determining the eligibility of the consumer concerned to receive access or continued access to classified information (as defined in section 604(b)(4)(E)(i)); and
(B) the agency or department certifies in writing to the person reselling the report that nondisclosure is necessary to protect classified information or the safety of persons employed by or contracting with, or undergoing investigation for work or contracting with the agency or department.
ß 608. Disclosures to governmental agencies [15 U.S.C. ß 1681f]
Notwithstanding the provisions of section 604 [ß 1681b] of this title, a consumer reporting agency may furnish identifying information respecting any consumer, limited to his name, address, former addresses, places of employ-

ment, or former places of employment, to a governmental agency.
ß 609. Disclosures to consumers [15 U.S.C. ß 1681g]
(a) Information on file; sources; report recipients. Every consumer reporting agency shall, upon request, and subject to 610(a)(1) [ß 1681h], clearly and accurately disclose to the consumer:
(1) All information in the consumer's file at the time of the request, except that nothing in this paragraph shall be construed to require a consumer reporting agency to disclose to a consumer any information concerning credit scores or any other risk scores or predictors relating to the consumer.
(2) The sources of the information; except that the sources of information acquired solely for use in preparing an investigative consumer report and actually used for no other purpose need not be disclosed: Provided, That in the event an action is brought under this title, such sources shall be available to the plaintiff under appropriate discovery procedures in the court in which the action is brought.
(3)(A) Identification of each person (including each end-user identified under section 607(e)(1) [ß 1681e]) that procured a consumer report
(i) for employment purposes, during the 2-year period preceding the date on which the request is made; or
(ii) for any other purpose, during the 1-year period preceding the date on which the request is made.
(B) An identification of a person under subparagraph (A) shall include
(i) the name of the person or, if applicable, the trade name (written in full) under which such person conducts business; and
(ii) upon request of the consumer, the address and telephone number of the person.
(C) Subparagraph (A) does not apply if—
(i) the end user is an agency or department of the United States Government that procures the report from the person for purposes of determining the eligibility of the consumer to whom the report relates to receive access or continued access to classified information (as defined in section 604(b)(4)(E)(i)); and
(ii) the head of the agency or department makes a written finding as prescribed under section 604(b)(4)(A).
(4) The dates, original payees, and amounts of any checks upon which is based any adverse characterization of the consumer, included in the file at the time of the disclosure.
(5) A record of all inquiries received by the agency during the 1-year period preceding the request that identified the consumer in connection with a credit or insurance transaction that was not initiated by the consumer.
(b) Exempt information. The requirements of subsection (a) of this section

respecting the disclosure of sources of information and the recipients of consumer reports do not apply to information received or consumer reports furnished prior to the effective date of this title except to the extent that the matter involved is contained in the files of the consumer reporting agency on that date.

(c) Summary of rights required to be included with disclosure.

(1) Summary of rights. A consumer reporting agency shall provide to a consumer, with each written disclosure by the agency to the consumer under this section

(A) a written summary of all of the rights that the consumer has under this title; and

(B) in the case of a consumer reporting agency that compiles and maintains files on consumers on a nationwide basis, a toll-free telephone number established by the agency, at which personnel are accessible to consumers during normal business hours.

(2) Specific items required to be included. The summary of rights required under paragraph (1) shall include

(A) a brief description of this title and all rights of consumers under this title;

(B) an explanation of how the consumer may exercise the rights of the consumer under this title;

(C) a list of all Federal agencies responsible for enforcing any provision of this title and the address and any appropriate phone number of each such agency, in a form that will assist the consumer in selecting the appropriate agency;

(D) a statement that the consumer may have additional rights under State law and that the consumer may wish to contact a State or local consumer protection agency or a State attorney general to learn of those rights; and

(E) a statement that a consumer reporting agency is not required to remove accurate derogatory information from a consumer's file, unless the information is outdated under section 605 [ß 1681c] or cannot be verified.

(3) Form of summary of rights. For purposes of this subsection and any disclosure by a consumer reporting agency required under this title with respect to consumers' rights, the Federal Trade Commission (after consultation with each Federal agency referred to in section 621(b) [ß 1681s]) shall prescribe the form and content of any such disclosure of the rights of consumers

required under this title. A consumer reporting agency shall be in compliance with this subsection if it provides disclosures under paragraph (1) that are substantially similar to the Federal Trade Commission prescription under this paragraph.

(4) Effectiveness. No disclosures shall be required under this subsection until the date on which the Federal Trade Commission prescribes the form and content of such disclosures under paragraph (3).

ß 610. Conditions and form of disclosure to consumers [15 U.S.C. ß 1681h]

(a) In general.

(1) Proper identification. A consumer reporting agency shall require, as a condition of making the disclosures required under section 609 [ß 1681g], that the consumer furnish proper identification.

(2) Disclosure in writing. Except as provided in subsection (b), the disclosures required to be made under section 609 [ß 1681g] shall be provided under that section in writing.

(b) Other forms of disclosure.

(1) In general. If authorized by a consumer, a consumer reporting agency may make the disclosures required under 609 [ß 1681g]

(A) other than in writing; and

(B) in such form as may be

(i) specified by the consumer in accordance with paragraph (2); and

(ii) available from the agency.

(2) Form. A consumer may specify pursuant to paragraph (1) that disclosures under section 609 [ß 1681g] shall be made

(A) in person, upon the appearance of the consumer at the place of business of the consumer reporting agency where disclosures are regularly provided, during normal business hours, and on reasonable notice;

(B) by telephone, if the consumer has made a written request for disclosure by telephone;

(C) by electronic means, if available from the agency; or

(D) by any other reasonable means that is available from the agency.

(c) Trained personnel. Any consumer reporting agency shall provide trained personnel to explain to the consumer any information furnished to him pursuant to section 609 [ß 1681g] of this title.

(d) Persons accompanying consumer. The consumer shall be permitted to be accompanied by one other person of his choosing, who shall furnish reason-

able identification. A consumer reporting agency may require the consumer to furnish a written statement granting permission to the consumer reporting agency to discuss the consumer's file in such person's presence.
(e) Limitation of liability. Except as provided in sections 616 and 617 [ßß 1681n and 1681o] of this title, no consumer may bring any action or proceeding in the nature of defamation, invasion of privacy, or negligence with respect to the reporting of information against any consumer reporting agency, any user of information, or any person who furnishes information to a consumer reporting agency, based on information disclosed pursuant to section 609, 610, or 615 [ßß 1681g, 1681h, or 1681m] of this title or based on information disclosed by a user of a consumer report to or for a consumer against whom the user has taken adverse action, based in whole or in part on the report, except as to false information furnished with malice or willful intent to injure such consumer.

ß 611. Procedure in case of disputed accuracy [15 U.S.C. ß 1681i]
(a) Reinvestigations of disputed information.
(1) Reinvestigation required.
(A) In general. If the completeness or accuracy of any item of information contained in a consumer's file at a consumer reporting agency is disputed by the consumer and the consumer notifies the agency directly of such dispute, the agency shall reinvestigate free of charge and record the current status of the disputed information, or delete the item from the file in accordance with paragraph (5), before the end of the 30-day period beginning on the date on which the agency receives the notice of the dispute from the consumer.
(B) Extension of period to reinvestigate. Except as provided in subparagraph (C), the 30-day period described in subparagraph (A) may be extended for not more than 15 additional days if the consumer reporting agency receives information from the consumer during that 30-day period that is relevant to the reinvestigation.
(C) Limitations on extension of period to reinvestigate. Subparagraph (B) shall not apply to any reinvestigation in which, during the 30-day period described in subparagraph (A), the information that is the subject of the reinvestigation is found to be inaccurate or incomplete or the consumer reporting agency determines that the information cannot be verified.
(2) Prompt notice of dispute to furnisher of information.
(A) In general. Before the expiration of the 5-business-day period beginning on the date on which a consumer reporting agency receives notice of a dispute from any consumer in accordance with paragraph (1), the agency shall provide notification of the dispute to any person who provided any item of information in dispute, at the address and in the manner established with the person. The

notice shall include all relevant information regarding the dispute that the agency has received from the consumer.

(B) Provision of other information from consumer. The consumer reporting agency shall promptly provide to the person who provided the information in dispute all relevant information regarding the dispute that is received by the agency from the consumer after the period referred to in subparagraph (A) and before the end of the period referred to in paragraph (1)(A).

(3) Determination that dispute is frivolous or irrelevant.

(A) In general. Notwithstanding paragraph (1), a consumer reporting agency may terminate a reinvestigation of information disputed by a consumer under that paragraph if the agency reasonably determines that the dispute by the consumer is frivolous or irrelevant, including by reason of a failure by a consumer to provide sufficient information to investigate the disputed information.

(B) Notice of determination. Upon making any determination in accordance with subparagraph (A) that a dispute is frivolous or irrelevant, a consumer reporting agency shall notify the consumer of such determination not later than 5 business days after making such determination, by mail or, if authorized by the consumer for that purpose, by any other means available to the agency.

(C) Contents of notice. A notice under subparagraph (B) shall include

(i) the reasons for the determination under subparagraph (A); and

(ii) identification of any information required to investigate the disputed information, which may consist of a standardized form describing the general nature of such information.

(4) Consideration of consumer information. In conducting any reinvestigation under paragraph (1) with respect to disputed information in the file of any consumer, the consumer reporting agency shall review and consider all relevant information submitted by the consumer in the period described in paragraph (1)(A) with respect to such disputed information.

(5) Treatment of inaccurate or unverifiable information.

(A) In general. If, after any reinvestigation under paragraph (1) of any information disputed by a consumer, an item of the information is found to be inaccurate or incomplete or cannot be verified, the consumer reporting agency shall promptly delete that item of information from the consumer's file or modify that item of information, as appropriate, based on the results of the reinvestigation.

(B) Requirements relating to reinsertion of previously deleted material.

(i) Certification of accuracy of information. If any information is deleted from a consumer's file pursuant to subparagraph (A), the information may not be rein-

serted in the file by the consumer reporting agency unless the person who furnishes the information certifies that the information is complete and accurate.
(ii) Notice to consumer. If any information that has been deleted from a consumer's file pursuant to subparagraph (A) is reinserted in the file, the consumer reporting agency shall notify the consumer of the reinsertion in writing not later than 5 business days after the reinsertion or, if authorized by the consumer for that purpose, by any other means available to the agency.
(iii) Additional information. As part of, or in addition to, the notice under clause (ii), a consumer reporting agency shall provide to a consumer in writing not later than 5 business days after the date of the reinsertion
(I) a statement that the disputed information has been reinserted;
(II) the business name and address of any furnisher of information contacted and the telephone number of such furnisher, if reasonably available, or of any furnisher of information that contacted the consumer reporting agency, in connection with the reinsertion of such information; and
(III) a notice that the consumer has the right to add a statement to the consumer's file disputing the accuracy or completeness of the disputed information.

C) Procedures to prevent reappearance. A consumer reporting agency shall maintain reasonable procedures designed to prevent the reappearance in a consumer's file, and in consumer reports on the consumer, of information that is deleted pursuant to this paragraph (other than information that is reinserted in accordance with subparagraph (B)(i)).
D) Automated reinvestigation system. Any consumer reporting agency that compiles and maintains files on consumers on a nationwide basis shall implement an automated system through which furnishers of information to that consumer reporting agency may report the results of a reinvestigation that finds incomplete or inaccurate information in a consumer's file to other such consumer reporting agencies.
(6) Notice of results of reinvestigation.
(A) In general. A consumer reporting agency shall provide written notice to a consumer of the results of a reinvestigation under this subsection not later than 5 business days after the completion of the reinvestigation, by mail or, if authorized by the consumer for that purpose, by other means available to the agency.
(B) Contents. As part of, or in addition to, the notice under subparagraph (A), a consumer reporting agency shall provide to a consumer in writing before the expiration of the 5-day period referred to in subparagraph (A)
(i) a statement that the reinvestigation is completed;

(ii) a consumer report that is based upon the consumer's file as that file is revised as a result of the reinvestigation;
(iii) a notice that, if requested by the consumer, a description of the procedure used to determine the accuracy and completeness of the information shall be provided to the consumer by the agency, including the business name and address of any furnisher of information contacted in connection with such information and the telephone number of such furnisher, if reasonably available;
(iv) a notice that the consumer has the right to add a statement to the consumer's file disputing the accuracy or completeness of the information; and
(v) a notice that the consumer has the right to request under subsection (d) that the consumer reporting agency furnish notifications under that subsection.
(7) Description of reinvestigation procedure. A consumer reporting agency shall provide to a consumer a description referred to in paragraph (6)(B)(iii) by not later than 15 days after receiving a request from the consumer for that description.
(8) Expedited dispute resolution. If a dispute regarding an item of information in a consumer's file at a consumer reporting agency is resolved in accordance with paragraph (5)(A) by the deletion of the disputed information by not later than 3 business days after the date on which the agency receives notice of the dispute from the consumer in accordance with paragraph (1)(A), then the agency shall not be required to comply with paragraphs (2), (6), and (7) with respect to that dispute if the agency
(A) provides prompt notice of the deletion to the consumer by telephone;
(B) includes in that notice, or in a written notice that accompanies a confirmation and consumer report provided in accordance with subparagraph (C), a statement of the consumer's right to request under subsection (d) that the agency furnish notifications under that subsection; and
(C) provides written confirmation of the deletion and a copy of a consumer report on the consumer that is based on the consumer's file after the deletion, not later than 5 business days after making the deletion.
(b) Statement of dispute. If the reinvestigation does not resolve the dispute, the consumer may file a brief statement setting forth the nature of the dispute. The consumer reporting agency may limit such statements to not more than one hundred words if it provides the consumer with assistance in writing a clear summary of the dispute.
(c) Notification of consumer dispute in subsequent consumer reports. Whenever a statement of a dispute is filed, unless there is reasonable grounds to believe that it is frivolous or irrelevant, the consumer reporting agency shall, in any subsequent consumer report containing the information in question, clearly note that it is disputed by the consumer and provide either the con-

sumer's statement or a clear and accurate codification or summary thereof.
(d) Notification of deletion of disputed information. Following any deletion of information which is found to be inaccurate or whose accuracy can no longer be verified or any notation as to disputed information, the consumer reporting agency shall, at the request of the consumer, furnish notification that the item has been deleted or the statement, codification or summary pursuant to subsection (b) or (c) of this section to any person specifically designated by the consumer who has within two years prior thereto received a consumer report for employment purposes, or within six months prior thereto received a consumer report for any other purpose, which contained the deleted or disputed information.

ß 612. Charges for certain disclosures [15 U.S.C. ß 1681j]

(a) Reasonable charges allowed for certain disclosures.

(1) In general. Except as provided in subsections (b), (c), and (d), a consumer reporting agency may impose a reasonable charge on a consumer

(A) for making a disclosure to the consumer pursuant to section 609 [ß 1681g], which charge

(i) shall not exceed $8;(3) and

(ii) shall be indicated to the consumer before making the disclosure; and

(B) for furnishing, pursuant to 611(d) [ß 1681i], following a reinvestigation under section 611(a) [ß 1681i], a statement, codification, or summary to a person designated by the consumer under that section after the 30-day period beginning on the date of notification of the consumer under paragraph (6) or (8) of section 611(a) [ß 1681i] with respect to the reinvestigation, which charge

(i) shall not exceed the charge that the agency would impose on each designated recipient for a consumer report; and

(ii) shall be indicated to the consumer before furnishing such information.

(2) Modification of amount. The Federal Trade Commission shall increase the amount referred to in paragraph (1)(A)(I) on January 1 of each year, based proportionally on changes in the Consumer Price Index, with fractional changes rounded to the nearest fifty cents.

(b) Free disclosure after adverse notice to consumer. Each consumer reporting agency that maintains a file on a consumer shall make all disclosures pursuant to section 609 [ß 1681g] without charge to the consumer if, not later than 60 days after receipt by such consumer of a notification pursuant to section 615 [ß 1681m], or of a notification from a debt collection agency affiliated with that consumer reporting agency stating that the consumer's credit rating may be or has been adversely affected, the consumer makes a request under section 609 [ß 1681g].

(c) Free disclosure under certain other circumstances. Upon the request of the consumer, a consumer reporting agency shall make all disclosures pursuant to section 609 [ß 1681g] once during any 12-month period without charge to that consumer if the consumer certifies in writing that the consumer
(1) is unemployed and intends to apply for employment in the 60-day period beginning on the date on which the certification is made;
(2) is a recipient of public welfare assistance; or
(3) has reason to believe that the file on the consumer at the agency contains inaccurate information due to fraud.
(d) Other charges prohibited. A consumer reporting agency shall not impose any charge on a consumer for providing any notification required by this title or making any disclosure required by this title, except as authorized by subsection (a).
ß 613. Public record information for employment purposes [15 U.S.C. ß 1681k]
(a) In general. A consumer reporting agency which furnishes a consumer report for employment purposes and which for that purpose compiles and reports items of information on consumers which are matters of public record and are likely to have an adverse effect upon a consumer's ability to obtain employment shall
(1) at the time such public record information is reported to the user of such consumer report, notify the consumer of the fact that public record information is being reported by the consumer reporting agency, together with the name and address of the person to whom such information is being reported; or
(2) maintain strict procedures designed to insure that whenever public record information which is likely to have an adverse effect on a consumer's ability to obtain employment is reported it is complete and up to date. For purposes of this paragraph, items of public record relating to arrests, indictments, convictions, suits, tax liens, and outstanding judgments shall be considered up to date if the current public record status of the item at the time of the report is reported.
(b) Exemption for national security investigations. Subsection (a) does not apply in the case of an agency or department of the United States Government that seeks to obtain and use a consumer report for employment purposes, if the head of the agency or department makes a written finding as prescribed under section 604(b)(4)(A).
ß 614. Restrictions on investigative consumer reports [15 U.S.C. ß 1681l]
Whenever a consumer reporting agency prepares an investigative consumer report, no adverse information in the consumer report (other than information

which is a matter of public record) may be included in a subsequent consumer report unless such adverse information has been verified in the process of making such subsequent consumer report, or the adverse information was received within the three-month period preceding the date the subsequent report is furnished.

ß 615. Requirements on users of consumer reports [15 U.S.C. ß 1681m]

(a) Duties of users taking adverse actions on the basis of information contained in consumer reports. If any person takes any adverse action with respect to any consumer that is based in whole or in part on any information contained in a consumer report, the person shall

(1) provide oral, written, or electronic notice of the adverse action to the consumer;

(2) provide to the consumer orally, in writing, or electronically

(A) the name, address, and telephone number of the consumer reporting agency (including a toll-free telephone number established by the agency if the agency compiles and maintains files on consumers on a nationwide basis) that furnished the report to the person; and

(B) a statement that the consumer reporting agency did not make the decision to take the adverse action and is unable to provide the consumer the specific reasons why the adverse action was taken; and

(3) provide to the consumer an oral, written, or electronic notice of the consumer's right

(A) to obtain, under section 612 [ß 1681j], a free copy of a consumer report on the consumer from the consumer reporting agency referred to in paragraph (2), which notice shall include an indication of the 60-day period under that section for obtaining such a copy; and

(B) to dispute, under section 611 [ß 1681i], with a consumer reporting agency the accuracy or completeness of any information in a consumer report furnished by the agency.

(b) Adverse action based on information obtained from third parties other than consumer reporting agencies.

(1) In general. Whenever credit for personal, family, or household purposes involving a consumer is denied or the charge for such credit is increased either wholly or partly because of information obtained from a person other than a consumer reporting agency bearing upon the consumer's credit worthiness, credit standing, credit capacity, character, general reputation, personal characteristics, or mode of living, the user of such information shall, within a reasonable period of time, upon the consumer's written request for the reasons for such adverse action received within sixty days after learning of such adverse action, disclose the nature of the information to the consumer. The

user of such information shall clearly and accurately disclose to the consumer his right to make such written request at the time such adverse action is communicated to the consumer.
(2) Duties of person taking certain actions based on information provided by affiliate.

(A) Duties, generally. If a person takes an action described in subparagraph (B) with respect to a consumer, based in whole or in part on information described in subparagraph (C), the person shall

(i) notify the consumer of the action, including a statement that the consumer may obtain the information in accordance with clause (ii); and

(ii) upon a written request from the consumer received within 60 days after transmittal of the notice required by clause (I), disclose to the consumer the nature of the information upon which the action is based by not later than 30 days after receipt of the request.
(B) Action described. An action referred to in subparagraph (A) is an adverse action described in section 603(k)(1)(A) [ß 1681a], taken in connection with a transaction initiated by the consumer, or any adverse action described in clause (i) or (ii) of section 603(k)(1)(B) [ß 1681a].
(C) Information described. Information referred to in subparagraph (A)
(i) except as provided in clause (ii), is information that

(I) is furnished to the person taking the action by a person related by common ownership or affiliated by common corporate control to the person taking the action; and
(II) bears on the credit worthiness, credit standing, credit capacity, character, general reputation, personal characteristics, or mode of living of the consumer; and

(ii) does not include
(I) information solely as to transactions or experiences between the consumer and the person furnishing the information; or
(II) information in a consumer report.
(c) Reasonable procedures to assure compliance. No person shall be held liable for any violation of this section if he shows by a preponderance of the evidence that at the time of the alleged violation he maintained reasonable procedures to assure compliance with the provisions of this section.

(d) Duties of users making written credit or insurance solicitations on the basis of information contained in consumer files.
(1) In general. Any person who uses a consumer report on any consumer in connection with any credit or insurance transaction that is not initiated by the consumer, that is provided to that person under section 604(c)(1)(B) [ß 1681b], shall provide with each written solicitation made to the consumer regarding the transaction a clear and conspicuous statement that
(A) information contained in the consumer's consumer report was used in connection with the transaction;
(B) the consumer received the offer of credit or insurance because the consumer satisfied the criteria for credit worthiness or insurability under which the consumer was selected for the offer;

(C) if applicable, the credit or insurance may not be extended if, after the consumer responds to the offer, the consumer does not meet the criteria used to select the consumer for the offer or any applicable criteria bearing on credit worthiness or insurability or does not furnish any required collateral;
(D) the consumer has a right to prohibit information contained in the consumer's file with any consumer reporting agency from being used in connection with any credit or insurance transaction that is not initiated by the consumer; and
(E) the consumer may exercise the right referred to in subparagraph (D) by notifying a notification system established under section 604(e) [ß 1681b].
(2) Disclosure of address and telephone number. A statement under paragraph (1) shall include the address and toll-free telephone number of the appropriate notification system established under section 604(e) [ß 1681b].
(3) Maintaining criteria on file. A person who makes an offer of credit or insurance to a consumer under a credit or insurance transaction described in paragraph (1) shall maintain on file the criteria used to select the consumer to receive the offer, all criteria bearing on credit worthiness or insurability, as applicable, that are the basis for determining whether or not to extend credit or insurance pursuant to the offer, and any requirement for the furnishing of collateral as a condition of the extension of credit or insurance, until the expiration of the 3-year period beginning on the date on which the offer is made to the consumer.
(4) Authority of federal agencies regarding unfair or deceptive acts or practices not affected. This section is not intended to affect the authority of any Federal or State agency to enforce a prohibition against unfair or deceptive acts or practices, including the making of false or misleading statements in connection with a credit or insurance transaction that is not initiated by the consumer.

ß 616. Civil liability for willful noncompliance [15 U.S.C. ß 1681n]
(a) In general. Any person who willfully fails to comply with any requirement imposed under this title with respect to any consumer is liable to that consumer in an amount equal to the sum of
(1)(A) any actual damages sustained by the consumer as a result of the failure or damages of not less than $100 and not more than $1,000; or
(B) in the case of liability of a natural person for obtaining a consumer report under false pretenses or knowingly without a permissible purpose, actual damages sustained by the consumer as a result of the failure or $1,000, whichever is greater;
(2) such amount of punitive damages as the court may allow; and
(3) in the case of any successful action to enforce any liability under this section, the costs of the action together with reasonable attorney's fees as determined by the court.
(b) Civil liability for knowing noncompliance. Any person who obtains a consumer report from a consumer reporting agency under false pretenses or knowingly without a permissible purpose shall be liable to the consumer reporting agency for actual damages sustained by the consumer reporting agency or $1,000, whichever is greater.
(c) Attorney's fees. Upon a finding by the court that an unsuccessful pleading, motion, or other paper filed in connection with an action under this section was filed in bad faith or for purposes of harassment, the court shall award to the prevailing party attorney's fees reasonable in relation to the work expended in responding to the pleading, motion, or other paper.
ß 617. Civil liability for negligent noncompliance [15 U.S.C. ß 1681o]
(a) In general. Any person who is negligent in failing to comply with any requirement imposed under this title with respect to any consumer is liable to that consumer in an amount equal to the sum of
(1) any actual damages sustained by the consumer as a result of the failure;
(2) in the case of any successful action to enforce any liability under this section, the costs of the action together with reasonable attorney's fees as determined by the court.
(b) Attorney's fees. On a finding by the court that an unsuccessful pleading, motion, or other paper filed in connection with an action under this section was filed in bad faith or for purposes of harassment, the court shall award to the prevailing party attorney's fees reasonable in relation to the work expended in responding to the pleading, motion, or other paper.
ß 618. Jurisdiction of courts; limitation of actions [15 U.S.C. ß 1681p]
An action to enforce any liability created under this title may be brought in any appropriate United States district court without regard to the amount in con-

troversy, or in any other court of competent jurisdiction, within two years from the date on which the liability arises, except that where a defendant has materially and willfully misrepresented any information required under this title to be disclosed to an individual and the information so misrepresented is material to the establishment of the defendant's liability to that individual under this title, the action may be brought at any time within two years after discovery by the individual of the misrepresentation.

ß 619. Obtaining information under false pretenses [15 U.S.C. ß 1681q]

Any person who knowingly and willfully obtains information on a consumer from a consumer reporting agency under false pretenses shall be fined under title 18, United States Code, imprisoned for not more than 2 years, or both.

ß 620. Unauthorized disclosures by officers or employees [15 U.S.C. ß 1681r]

Any officer or employee of a consumer reporting agency who knowingly and willfully provides information concerning an individual from the agency's files to a person not authorized to receive that information shall be fined under title 18, United States Code, imprisoned for not more than 2 years, or both.

ß 621. Administrative enforcement [15 U.S.C. ß 1681s]

(a) (1) Enforcement by Federal Trade Commission. Compliance with the requirements imposed under this title shall be enforced under the Federal Trade Commission Act [15 U.S.C. ßß 41 et seq.] by the Federal Trade Commission with respect to consumer reporting agencies and all other persons subject thereto, except to the extent that enforcement of the requirements imposed under this title is specifically committed to some other government agency under subsection (b) hereof. For the purpose of the exercise by the Federal Trade Commission of its functions and powers under the Federal Trade Commission Act, a violation of any requirement or prohibition imposed under this title shall constitute an unfair or deceptive act or practice in commerce in violation of section 5(a) of the Federal Trade Commission Act [15 U.S.C. ß 45(a)] and shall be subject to enforcement by the Federal Trade Commission under section 5(b) thereof [15 U.S.C. ß 45(b)] with respect to any consumer reporting agency or person subject to enforcement by the Federal Trade Commission pursuant to this subsection, irrespective of whether that person is engaged in commerce or meets any other jurisdictional tests in the Federal Trade Commission Act. The Federal Trade Commission shall have such procedural, investigative, and enforcement powers, including the power to issue procedural rules in enforcing compliance with the requirements imposed under this title and to require the filing of reports, the production of documents, and the appearance of witnesses as though the applicable terms and conditions of the Federal Trade Commission Act were part of this title. Any person violating any of the provisions of this title shall be subject to the penalties and entitled to the privileges and immunities provided in the Federal Trade Commission Act as though the applicable terms and provisions thereof were part of this title.

(2)(A) In the event of a knowing violation, which constitutes a pattern or practice of violations of this title, the Commission may commence a civil action to recover a civil penalty in a district court of the United States against any person that violates this title. In such action, such person shall be liable for a civil penalty of not more than $2,500 per violation.

(B) In determining the amount of a civil penalty under subparagraph (A), the court shall take into account the degree of culpability, any history of prior such conduct, ability to pay, effect on ability to continue to do business, and such other matters as justice may require.

(3) Notwithstanding paragraph (2), a court may not impose any civil penalty on a person for a violation of section 623(a)(1) [ß 1681s-2] unless the person has been enjoined from committing the violation, or ordered not to commit the violation, in an action or proceeding brought by or on behalf of the Federal Trade Commission, and has violated the injunction or order, and the court may not impose any civil penalty for any violation occurring before the date of the violation of the injunction or order.

(b) Enforcement by other agencies. Compliance with the requirements imposed under this title with respect to consumer reporting agencies, persons who use consumer reports from such agencies, persons who furnish information to such agencies, and users of information that are subject to subsection (d) of section 615 [ß 1681m] shall be enforced under

(1) section 8 of the Federal Deposit Insurance Act [12 U.S.C. ß 1818], in the case of

(A) national banks, and Federal branches and Federal agencies of foreign banks, by the Office of the Comptroller of the Currency;

(B) member banks of the Federal Reserve System (other than national banks), branches and agencies of foreign banks (other than Federal branches, Federal agencies, and insured State branches of foreign banks), commercial lending companies owned or controlled by foreign banks, and organizations operating under section 25 or 25(a) [25A] of the Federal Reserve Act [12 U.S.C. ßß 601 et seq., ßß 611 et seq], by the Board of Governors of the Federal Reserve System; and

(C) banks insured by the Federal Deposit Insurance Corporation (other than members of the Federal Reserve System) and insured State branches of foreign banks, by the Board of Directors of the Federal Deposit Insurance

Corporation;

(2) section 8 of the Federal Deposit Insurance Act [12 U.S.C. ß 1818], by the Director of the Office of Thrift Supervision, in the case of a savings association the deposits of which are insured by the Federal Deposit Insurance Corporation;

(3) the Federal Credit Union Act [12 U.S.C. ßß 1751 et seq.], by the Administrator of the National Credit Union Administration [National Credit Union Administration Board] with respect to any Federal credit union;

(4) subtitle IV of title 49 [49 U.S.C. ßß 10101 et seq.], by the Secretary of Transportation, with respect to all carriers subject to the jurisdiction of the Surface Transportation Board;

(5) the Federal Aviation Act of 1958 [49 U.S.C. Appx ßß 1301 et seq.], by the Secretary of Transportation with respect to any air carrier or foreign air carrier subject to that Act [49 U.S.C. Appx ßß 1301 et seq.]; and

(6) the Packers and Stockyards Act, 1921 [7 U.S.C. ßß 181 et seq.] (except as provided in section 406 of that Act [7 U.S.C. ßß 226 and 227]), by the Secretary of Agriculture with respect to any activities subject to that Act.

The terms used in paragraph (1) that are not defined in this title or otherwise defined in section 3(s) of the Federal Deposit Insurance Act (12 U.S.C. ß1813(s)) shall have the meaning given to them in section 1(b) of the International Banking Act of 1978 (12 U.S.C. ß 3101).

(c) State action for violations.

(1) Authority of states. In addition to such other remedies as are provided under State law, if the chief law enforcement officer of a State, or an official or agency designated by a State, has reason to believe that any person has violated or is violating this title, the State

(A) may bring an action to enjoin such violation in any appropriate United States district court or in any other court of competent jurisdiction;

(B) subject to paragraph (5), may bring an action on behalf of the residents of the State to recover

(i) damages for which the person is liable to such residents under sections 616 and 617 [ßß 1681n and 1681o] as a result of the violation;

(ii) in the case of a violation of section 623(a) [ß 1681s-2], damages for which the person would, but for section 623(c) [ß 1681s-2], be liable to such residents as a result of the violation; or

(iii) damages of not more than $1,000 for each willful or negligent violation; and

(C) in the case of any successful action under subparagraph (A) or (B), shall be awarded the costs of the action and reasonable attorney fees as determined by the court.

(2) Rights of federal regulators. The State shall serve prior written notice of any action under paragraph (1) upon the Federal Trade Commission or the appropriate Federal regulator determined under subsection (b) and provide the Commission or appropriate Federal regulator with a copy of its complaint, except in any case in which such prior notice is not feasible, in which case the State shall serve such notice immediately upon instituting such action. The Federal Trade Commission or appropriate Federal regulator shall have the right
(A) to intervene in the action;
(B) upon so intervening, to be heard on all matters arising therein;
(C) to remove the action to the appropriate United States district court; and
(D) to file petitions for appeal.
(3) Investigatory powers. For purposes of bringing any action under this subsection, nothing in this subsection shall prevent the chief law enforcement officer, or an official or agency designated by a State, from exercising the powers conferred on the chief law enforcement officer or such official by the laws of such State to conduct investigations or to administer oaths or affirmations or to compel the attendance of witnesses or the production of documentary and other evidence.
(4) Limitation on state action while federal action pending. If the Federal Trade Commission or the appropriate Federal regulator has instituted a civil action or an administrative action under section 8 of the Federal Deposit Insurance Act for a violation of this title, no State may, during the pendency of such action, bring an action under this section against any defendant named in the complaint of the Commission or the appropriate Federal regulator for any violation of this title that is alleged in that complaint.

(5) Limitations on state actions for violation of section 623(a)(1) [ß 1681s-2].
(A) Violation of injunction required. A State may not bring an action against a person under paragraph (1)(B) for a violation of section 623(a)(1) [ß 1681s-2], unless
(i) the person has been enjoined from committing the violation, in an action brought by the State under paragraph (1)(A); and
(ii) the person has violated the injunction.

(B) Limitation on damages recoverable. In an action against a person under paragraph (1)(B) for a violation of section 623(a)(1) [ß 1681s-2], a State may not recover any damages incurred before the date of the violation of an injunction on which the action is based.

(d) Enforcement under other authority. For the purpose of the exercise by any agency referred to in subsection (b) of this section of its powers under any Act referred to in that subsection, a violation of any requirement imposed under this title shall be deemed to be a violation of a requirement imposed under that Act. In addition to its powers under any provision of law specifically referred to in subsection (b) of this section, each of the agencies referred to in that subsection may exercise, for the purpose of enforcing compliance with any requirement imposed under this title any other authority conferred on it by law.

(e) Regulatory authority

(1) The Federal banking agencies referred to in paragraphs (1) and (2) of subsection (b) shall jointly prescribe such regulations as necessary to carry out the purposes of this Act with respect to any persons identified under paragraphs (1) and (2) of subsection (b), and the Board of Governors of the Federal Reserve System shall have authority to prescribe regulations consistent with such joint regulations with respect to bank holding companies and affiliates (other than depository institutions and consumer reporting agencies) of such holding companies.

(2) The Board of the National Credit Union Administration shall prescribe such regulations as necessary to carry out the purposes of this Act with respect to any persons identified under paragraph (3) of subsection (b).

ß 622. Information on overdue child support obligations [15 U.S.C. ß 1681s-1]

Notwithstanding any other provision of this title, a consumer reporting agency shall include in any consumer report furnished by the agency in accordance with section 604 [ß 1681b] of this title, any information on the failure of the consumer to pay overdue support which

(1) is provided

(A) to the consumer reporting agency by a State or local child support enforcement agency; or

(B) to the consumer reporting agency and verified by any local, State, or Federal government agency; and

(2) antedates the report by 7 years or less.

ß 623. Responsibilities of furnishers of information to consumer reporting agencies [15 U.S.C. ß 1681s-2]

(a) Duty of furnishers of information to provide accurate information.

(1) Prohibition.

(A) Reporting information with actual knowledge of errors. A person shall not furnish any information relating to a consumer to any consumer reporting agency if the person knows or consciously avoids knowing that the information is inaccurate.
(B) Reporting information after notice and confirmation of errors. A person shall not furnish information relating to a consumer to any consumer reporting agency if
(i) the person has been notified by the consumer, at the address specified by the person for such notices, that specific information is inaccurate; and
(ii) the information is, in fact, inaccurate.
(C) No address requirement. A person who clearly and conspicuously specifies to the consumer an address for notices referred to in subparagraph (B) shall not be subject to subparagraph (A); however, nothing in subparagraph (B) shall require a person to specify such an address.
(2) Duty to correct and update information. A person who
(A) regularly and in the ordinary course of business furnishes information to one or more consumer reporting agencies about the person's transactions or experiences with any consumer; and
(B) has furnished to a consumer reporting agency information that the person determines is not complete or accurate, shall promptly notify the consumer reporting agency of that determination and provide to the agency any corrections to that information, or any additional information, that is necessary to make the information provided by the person to the agency complete and accurate, and shall not thereafter furnish to the agency any of the information that remains not complete or accurate.
(3) Duty to provide notice of dispute. If the completeness or accuracy of any information furnished by any person to any consumer reporting agency is disputed to such person by a consumer, the person may not furnish the information to any consumer reporting agency without notice that such information is disputed by the consumer.
(4) Duty to provide notice of closed accounts. A person who regularly and in the ordinary course of business furnishes information to a consumer reporting agency regarding a consumer who has a credit account with that person shall notify the agency of the voluntary closure of the account by the consumer, in information regularly furnished for the period in which the account is closed.
(5) Duty to provide notice of delinquency of accounts. A person who furnishes information to a consumer reporting agency regarding a delinquent account being placed for collection, charged to profit or loss, or subjected to any similar action shall, not later than 90 days after furnishing the information, notify the agency of the month and year of the commencement of the delinquency

that immediately preceded the action.
(b) Duties of furnishers of information upon notice of dispute.
(1) In general. After receiving notice pursuant to section 611(a)(2) [ß 1681i] of a dispute with regard to the completeness or accuracy of any information provided by a person to a consumer reporting agency, the person shall
(A) conduct an investigation with respect to the disputed information;
(B) review all relevant information provided by the consumer reporting agency pursuant to section 611(a)(2) [ß 1681i];
(C) report the results of the investigation to the consumer reporting agency; and
(D) if the investigation finds that the information is incomplete or inaccurate, report those results to all other consumer reporting agencies to which the person furnished the information and that compile and maintain files on consumers on a nationwide basis.
(2) Deadline. A person shall complete all investigations, reviews, and reports required under paragraph (1) regarding information provided by the person to a consumer reporting agency, before the expiration of the period under section 611(a)(1) [ß 1681i] within which the consumer reporting agency is required to complete actions required by that section regarding that information.
(c) Limitation on liability. Sections 616 and 617 [ßß 1681n and 1681o] do not apply to any failure to comply with subsection (a), except as provided in section 621(c)(1)(B) [ß 1681s].
(d) Limitation on enforcement. Subsection (a) shall be enforced exclusively under section 621 [ß 1681s] by the Federal agencies and officials and the State officials identified in that section.
ß 624. Relation to State laws [15 U.S.C. ß 1681t]
(a) In general. Except as provided in subsections (b) and (c), this title does not annul, alter, affect, or exempt any person subject to the provisions of this title from complying with the laws of any State with respect to the collection, distribution, or use of any information on consumers, except to the extent that those laws are inconsistent with any provision of this title, and then only to the extent of the inconsistency.
(b) General exceptions. No requirement or prohibition may be imposed under the laws of any State
(1) with respect to any subject matter regulated under
(A) subsection (c) or (e) of section 604 [ß 1681b], relating to the prescreening of consumer reports;
(B) section 611 [ß 1681i], relating to the time by which a consumer reporting agency must take any action, including the provision of notification to a consumer or other person, in any procedure related to the disputed accuracy of

information in a consumer's file, except that this subparagraph shall not apply to any State law in effect on the date of enactment of the Consumer Credit Reporting Reform Act of 1996;
(C) subsections (a) and (b) of section 615 [ß 1681m], relating to the duties of a person who takes any adverse action with respect to a consumer;
(D) section 615(d) [ß 1681m], relating to the duties of persons who use a consumer report of a consumer in connection with any credit or insurance transaction that is not initiated by the consumer and that consists of a firm offer of credit or insurance;
(E) section 605 [ß 1681c], relating to information contained in consumer reports, except that this subparagraph shall not apply to any State law in effect on the date of enactment of the Consumer Credit Reporting Reform Act of 1996; or
(F) section 623 [ß 1681s-2], relating to the responsibilities of persons who furnish information to consumer reporting agencies, except that this paragraph shall not apply
(i) with respect to section 54A(a) of chapter 93 of the Massachusetts Annotated Laws (as in effect on the date of enactment of the Consumer Credit Reporting Reform Act of 1996); or
(ii) with respect to section 1785.25(a) of the California Civil Code (as in effect on the date of enactment of the Consumer Credit Reporting Reform Act of 1996);
(2) with respect to the exchange of information among persons affiliated by common ownership or common corporate control, except that this paragraph shall not apply with respect to subsection (a) or (c)(1) of section 2480e of title 9, Vermont Statutes Annotated (as in effect on the date of enactment of the Consumer Credit Reporting Reform Act of 1996); or
(3) with respect to the form and content of any disclosure required to be made under section 609(c) [ß 1681g].
(c) Definition of firm offer of credit or insurance. Notwithstanding any definition of the term "firm offer of credit or insurance" (or any equivalent term) under the laws of any State, the definition of that term contained in section 603(l) [ß 1681a] shall be construed to apply in the enforcement and interpretation of the laws of any State governing consumer reports.
(d) Limitations. Subsections (b) and (c)
(1) do not affect any settlement, agreement, or consent judgment between any State Attorney General and any consumer reporting agency in effect on the date of enactment of the Consumer Credit Reporting Reform Act of 1996; and
(2) do not apply to any provision of State law (including any provision of a State constitution) that

(A) is enacted after January 1, 2004;
(B) states explicitly that the provision is intended to supplement this title; and
(C) gives greater protection to consumers than is provided under this title.
ß 625. Disclosures to FBI for counterintelligence purposes [15 U.S.C. ß 1681u]
(a) Identity of financial institutions. Notwithstanding section 604 [ß 1681b] or any other provision of this title, a consumer reporting agency shall furnish to the Federal Bureau of Investigation the names and addresses of all financial institutions (as that term is defined in section 1101 of the Right to Financial Privacy Act of 1978 [12 U.S.C. ß 3401]) at which a consumer maintains or has maintained an account, to the extent that information is in the files of the agency, when presented with a written request for that information, signed by the Director of the Federal Bureau of Investigation, or the Director's designee in a position not lower than Deputy Assistant Director at Bureau headquarters or a Special Agent in Charge of a Bureau field office designated by the Director, which certifies compliance with this section. The Director or the Director's designee may make such a certification only if the Director or the Director's designee has determined in writing, that such information is sought for the conduct of an authorized investigation to protect against international terrorism or clandestine intelligence activities, provided that such an investigation of a United States person is not conducted solely upon the basis of activities protected by the first amendment to the Constitution of the United States.
(b) Identifying information. Notwithstanding the provisions of section 604 [ß 1681b] or any other provision of this title, a consumer reporting agency shall furnish identifying information respecting a consumer, limited to name, address, former addresses, places of employment, or former places of employment, to the Federal Bureau of Investigation when presented with a written request, signed by the Director or the Director's designee, which certifies compliance with this subsection. The Director or the Director's designee in a position not lower than Deputy Assistant Director at Bureau headquarters or a Special Agent in Charge of a Bureau field office designated by the Director may make such a certification only if the Director or the Director's designee has determined in writing that such information is sought for the conduct of an authorized investigation to protect against international terrorism or clandestine intelligence activities, provided that such an investigation of a United States person is not conducted solely upon the basis of activities protected by the first amendment to the Constitution of the United States.
(c) Court order for disclosure of consumer reports. Notwithstanding section 604 [ß 1681b] or any other provision of this title, if requested in writing by the Director of the Federal Bureau of Investigation, or a designee of the Director

in a position not lower than Deputy Assistant Director at Bureau headquarters or a Special Agent in Charge of a Bureau field office designated by the Director, a court may issue an order ex parte directing a consumer reporting agency to furnish a consumer report to the Federal Bureau of Investigation, upon a showing in camera that the consumer report is sought for the conduct of an authorized investigation to protect against international terrorism or clandestine intelligence activities, provided that such an investigation of a United States person is not conducted solely upon the basis of activities protected by the first amendment to the Constitution of the United States.

The terms of an order issued under this subsection shall not disclose that the order is issued for purposes of a counterintelligence investigation.

(d) Confidentiality. No consumer reporting agency or officer, employee, or agent of a consumer reporting agency shall disclose to any person, other than those officers, employees, or agents of a consumer reporting agency necessary to fulfill the requirement to disclose information to the Federal Bureau of Investigation under this section, that the Federal Bureau of Investigation has sought or obtained the identity of financial institutions or a consumer report respecting any consumer under subsection (a), (b), or (c), and no consumer reporting agency or officer, employee, or agent of a consumer reporting agency shall include in any consumer report any information that would indicate that the Federal Bureau of Investigation has sought or obtained such information or a consumer report.

(e) Payment of fees. The Federal Bureau of Investigation shall, subject to the availability of appropriations, pay to the consumer reporting agency assembling or providing report or information in accordance with procedures established under this section a fee for reimbursement for such costs as are reasonably necessary and which have been directly incurred in searching, reproducing, or transporting books, papers, records, or other data required or requested to be produced under this section.

(f) Limit on dissemination. The Federal Bureau of Investigation may not disseminate information obtained pursuant to this section outside of the Federal Bureau of Investigation, except to other Federal agencies as may be necessary for the approval or conduct of a foreign counterintelligence investigation, or, where the information concerns a person subject to the Uniform Code of Military Justice, to appropriate investigative authorities within the military department concerned as may be necessary for the conduct of a joint foreign counterintelligence investigation.

(g) Rules of construction. Nothing in this section shall be construed to prohibit information from being furnished by the Federal Bureau of Investigation pursuant to a subpoena or court order, in connection with a judicial or administrative proceeding to enforce the provisions of this Act. Nothing in this section shall be construed to authorize or permit the withholding of information from the Congress.

(h) Reports to Congress. On a semiannual basis, the Attorney General shall fully inform the Permanent Select Committee on Intelligence and the Committee on Banking, Finance and Urban Affairs of the House of Representatives, and the Select Committee on Intelligence and the Committee on Banking, Housing, and Urban Affairs of the Senate concerning all requests made pursuant to subsections (a), (b), and (c).

(i) Damages. Any agency or department of the United States obtaining or disclosing any consumer reports, records, or information contained therein in violation of this section is liable to the consumer to whom such consumer reports, records, or information relate in an amount equal to the sum of

(1) $100, without regard to the volume of consumer reports, records, or information involved;

(2) any actual damages sustained by the consumer as a result of the disclosure;

(3) if the violation is found to have been willful or intentional, such punitive damages as a court may allow; and

(4) in the case of any successful action to enforce liability under this subsection, the costs of the action, together with reasonable attorney fees, as determined by the court.

(j) Disciplinary actions for violations. If a court determines that any agency or department of the United States has violated any provision of this section and the court finds that the circumstances surrounding the violation raise questions of whether or not an officer or employee of the agency or department acted willfully or intentionally with respect to the violation, the agency or department shall promptly initiate a proceeding to determine whether or not disciplinary action is warranted against the officer or employee who was responsible for the violation.

(k) Good-faith exception. Notwithstanding any other provision of this title, any consumer reporting agency or agent or employee thereof making disclosure of consumer reports or identifying information pursuant to this subsection in good-faith reliance upon a certification of the Federal Bureau of Investigation pursuant to provisions of this section shall not be liable to any person for such disclosure under this title, the constitution of any State, or any law or regulation of any State or any political subdivision of any State.

(l) Limitation of remedies. Notwithstanding any other provision of this title, the remedies and sanctions set forth in this section shall be the only judicial remedies and sanctions for violation of this section.

(m) Injunctive relief. In addition to any other remedy contained in this section, injunctive relief shall be available to require compliance with the procedures of this section. In the event of any successful action under this subsection, costs together with reasonable attorney fees, as determined by the court, may be recovered.

ß 626. Disclosures to governmental agencies for counterterrorism purposes [15 U.S.C. ß1681v]

(a) Disclosure. Notwithstanding section 604 or any other provision of this title, a consumer reporting agency shall furnish a consumer report of a consumer and all other information in a consumer's file to a government agency authorized to conduct investigations of, or intelligence or counterintelligence activities or analysis related to, international terrorism when presented with a written certification by such government agency that such information is necessary for the agency's conduct or such investigation, activity or analysis.

(b) Form of certification. The certification described in subsection (a) shall be signed by a supervisory official designated by the head of a Federal agency or an officer of a Federal agency whose appointment to office is required to be made by the President, by and with the advice and consent of the Senate.

(c) Confidentiality. No consumer reporting agency, or officer, employee, or agent of such consumer reporting agency, shall disclose to any person, or specify in any consumer report, that a government agency has sought or obtained access to information under subsection (a).

(d) Rule of construction. Nothing in section 625 shall be construed to limit the authority of the Director of the Federal Bureau of Investigation under this section.

(e) Safe harbor. Notwithstanding any other provision of this title, any consumer reporting agency or agent or employee thereof making disclosure of consumer reports or other information pursuant to this section in good-faith reliance upon a certification of a governmental agency pursuant to the provisions of this section shall not be liable to any person for such disclosure under this subchapter, the constitution of any State, or any law or regulation of any State or any political subdivision of any State.

Legislative History
House Reports:
No. 91-975 (Comm. on Banking and Currency) and
No. 91-1587 (Comm. of Conference)
Senate Reports:
No. 91-1139 accompanying S. 3678 (Comm. on Banking and Currency)
Congressional Record, Vol. 116 (1970)

May 25, considered and passed House.
Sept. 18, considered and passed Senate, amended.
Oct. 9, Senate agreed to conference report.
Oct. 13, House agreed to conference report.
Enactment:
Public Law No. 91-508 (October 26, 1970):
Amendments: Public Law Nos.
95-473 (October 17, 1978)
95-598 (November 6, 1978)
98-443 (October 4, 1984)
101-73 (August 9, 1989)
102-242 (December 19, 1991)
102-537 (October 27, 1992)
102-550 (October 28, 1992)
103-325 (September 23, 1994)
104-88 (December 29, 1995)
104-93 (January 6, 1996)
104-193 (August 22, 1996)
104-208 (September 30, 1996)
105-107 (November 20, 1997)
105-347 (November 2, 1998)
106-102 (November 12, 1999)
107-56 (October 26, 2001)
Endnotes:
1. The reporting periods have been lengthened for certain adverse information pertaining to U.S. Government insured or guaranteed student loans, or pertaining to national direct student loans. See sections 430A(f) and 463(c)(3) of the Higher Education Act of 1965, 20 U.S.C. 1080a(f) and 20 U.S.C. 1087cc(c)(3), respectively.
2. Should read "paragraphs (4) and (5)...." Prior Section 605(a)(6) was amended and re-designated as Section 605(a)(5) in November 1998.
3. The Federal Trade Commission increased the maximum allowable charge to $9.00, effective January 1, 2002. 66 Fed. Reg. 63545 (Dec. 7, 2001).

THE FAIR DEBT COLLECTION PRACTICES ACT
As amended by Public Law 104-208, 110 Stat. 3009 (Sept. 30, 1996)

To amend the Consumer Credit Protection Act to prohibit abusive practices by debt collectors.

Be it enacted by the Senate and House of Representatives of the United States of America in Congress assembled, That the Consumer Credit Protection Act (15 U.S.C. 1601 et seq.) is amended by adding at the end thereof the following new title:

TITLE VIII - DEBT COLLECTION PRACTICES [Fair Debt Collection Practices Act]

Sec.

801. Short Title
802. Congressional findings and declaration of purpose
803. Definitions
804. Acquisition of location information
805. Communication in connection with debt collection
806. Harassment or abuse
807. False or misleading representations
808. Unfair practice
809. Validation of debts
810. Multiple debts
811. Legal actions by debt collectors
812. Furnishing certain deceptive forms
813. Civil liability
814. Administrative enforcement
815. Reports to Congress by the Commission
816. Relation to State laws
817. Exemption for State regulation
818. Effective date

ß 801. Short Title [15 USC 1601 note]

This title may be cited as the "Fair Debt Collection Practices Act."

ß 802. Congressional findings and declarations of purpose [15 USC 1692]

(a) There is abundant evidence of the use of abusive, deceptive, and unfair debt collection practices by many debt collectors. Abusive debt collection practices contribute to the number of personal bankruptcies, to marital instability, to the loss of jobs, and to invasions of individual privacy.

(b) Existing laws and procedures for redressing these injuries are inadequate to protect consumers.

(c) Means other than misrepresentation or other abusive debt collection practices are available for the effective collection of debts.

(d) Abusive debt collection practices are carried on to a substantial extent in interstate commerce and through means and instrumentalities of such commerce. Even where abusive debt collection practices are purely intrastate in character, they nevertheless directly affect interstate commerce.

(e) It is the purpose of this title to eliminate abusive debt collection practices by debt collectors, to insure that those debt collectors who refrain from using abusive debt collection practices are not competitively disadvantaged, and to promote consistent State action to protect consumers against debt collection abuses.

ß 803. Definitions [15 USC 1692a]

As used in this title –

(1) The term "Commission" means the Federal Trade Commission.

(2) The term "communication" means the conveying of information regarding a debt directly or indirectly to any person through any medium.

(3) The term "consumer" means any natural person obligated or allegedly obligated to pay any debt.

(4) The term "creditor" means any person who offers or extends credit creating a debt or to whom a debt is owed, but such term does not include any person to the extent that he receives an assignment or transfer of a debt in default solely for the purpose of facilitating collection of such debt for another.

(5) The term "debt" means any obligation or alleged obligation of a consumer to pay money arising out of a transaction in which the money, property, insurance or services which are the subject of the transaction are primarily for personal, family, or household purposes, whether or not such obligation has been reduced to judgment.

(6) The term "debt collector" means any person who uses any instrumentality of interstate commerce or the mails in any business the principal purpose of which is the collection of any debts, or who regularly collects or attempts to collect, directly or indirectly, debts owed or due or asserted to be owed or due another. Notwithstanding the exclusion provided by clause (F) of the last sentence of this paragraph, the term includes any creditor who, in the process of collecting his own debts, uses any name other than his own which would indicate that a third person is collecting or attempting to collect such debts. For the purpose of section 808(6), such term also includes any person who uses any instrumentality of interstate commerce or the mails in any business the principal purpose of which is the enforcement of security interests. The term does not include –

(A) any officer or employee of a creditor while, in the name of the creditor, collecting debts for such creditor;

(B) any person while acting as a debt collector for another person, both of whom are related by common ownership or affiliated by corporate control, if the person acting as a debt collector does so only for persons to whom it is so related or affiliated and if the principal business of such person is not the collection of debts;

(C) any officer or employee of the United States or any State to the extent that collecting or attempting to collect any debt is in the performance of his official duties;
(D) any person while serving or attempting to serve legal process on any other person in connection with the judicial enforcement of any debt;
(E) any nonprofit organization which, at the request of consumers, performs bona fide consumer credit counseling and assists consumers in the liquidation of their debts by receiving payments from such consumers and distributing such amounts to creditors; and
(F) any person collecting or attempting to collect any debt owed or due or asserted to be owed or due another to the extent such activity (i) is incidental to a bona fide fiduciary obligation or a bona fide escrow arrangement; (ii) concerns a debt which was originated by such person; (iii) concerns a debt which was not in default at the time it was obtained by such person; or (iv) concerns a debt obtained by such person as a secured party in a commercial credit transaction involving the creditor.
(7) The term "location information" means a consumer's place of abode and his telephone number at such place, or his place of employment.
(8) The term "State" means any State, territory, or possession of the United States, the District of Columbia, the Commonwealth of Puerto Rico, or any political subdivision of any of the foregoing.
ß 804. Acquisition of location information [15 USC 1692b]
Any debt collector communicating with any person other than the consumer for the purpose of acquiring location information about the consumer shall —
(1) identify himself, state that he is confirming or correcting location information concerning the consumer, and, only if expressly requested, identify his employer;
(2) not state that such consumer owes any debt;
(3) not communicate with any such person more than once unless requested to do so by such person or unless the debt collector reasonably believes that the earlier response of such person is erroneous or incomplete and that such person now has correct or complete location information;
(4) not communicate by post card;
(5) not use any language or symbol on any envelope or in the contents of any communication effected by the mails or telegram that indicates that the debt collector is in the debt collection business or that the communication relates to the collection of a debt; and
(6) after the debt collector knows the consumer is represented by an attorney with regard to the subject debt and has knowledge of, or can readily ascertain, such attorney's name and address, not communicate with any person other

than that attorney, unless the attorney fails to respond within a reasonable period of time to the communication from the debt collector.

ß 805. Communication in connection with debt collection [15 USC 1692c]

(a) COMMUNICATION WITH THE CONSUMER GENERALLY. Without the prior consent of the consumer given directly to the debt collector or the express permission of a court of competent jurisdiction, a debt collector may not communicate with a consumer in connection with the collection of any debt —

(1) at any unusual time or place or a time or place known or which should be known to be inconvenient to the consumer. In the absence of knowledge of circumstances to the contrary, a debt collector shall assume that the convenient time for communicating with a consumer is after 8 o'clock antimeridian and before 9 o'clock postmeridian, local time at the consumer's location;

(2) if the debt collector knows the consumer is represented by an attorney with respect to such debt and has knowledge of, or can readily ascertain, such attorney's name and address, unless the attorney fails to respond within a reasonable period of time to a communication from the debt collector or unless the attorney consents to direct communication with the consumer; or

(3) at the consumer's place of employment if the debt collector knows or has reason to know that the consumer's employer prohibits the consumer from receiving such communication.

(b) COMMUNICATION WITH THIRD PARTIES. Except as provided in section 804, without the prior consent of the consumer given directly to the debt collector, or the express permission of a court of competent jurisdiction, or as reasonably necessary to effectuate a postjudgment judicial remedy, a debt collector may not communicate, in connection with the collection of any debt, with any person other than a consumer, his attorney, a consumer reporting agency if otherwise permitted by law, the creditor, the attorney of the creditor, or the attorney of the debt collector.

(c) CEASING COMMUNICATION. If a consumer notifies a debt collector in writing that the consumer refuses to pay a debt or that the consumer wishes the debt collector to cease further communication with the consumer, the debt collector shall not communicate further with the consumer with respect to such debt, except —

(1) to advise the consumer that the debt collector's further efforts are being terminated;

(2) to notify the consumer that the debt collector or creditor may invoke specified remedies which are ordinarily invoked by such debt collector or creditor; or

(3) where applicable, to notify the consumer that the debt collector or creditor intends to invoke a specified remedy.

If such notice from the consumer is made by mail, notification shall be complete upon receipt.

(d) For the purpose of this section, the term "consumer" includes the consumer's spouse, parent (if the consumer is a minor), guardian, executor, or administrator.

ß 806. Harassment or abuse [15 USC 1692d]

A debt collector may not engage in any conduct the natural consequence of which is to harass, oppress, or abuse any person in connection with the collection of a debt. Without limiting the general application of the foregoing, the following conduct is a violation of this section:

(1) The use or threat of use of violence or other criminal means to harm the physical person, reputation, or property of any person.

(2) The use of obscene or profane language or language the natural consequence of which is to abuse the hearer or reader.

(3) The publication of a list of consumers who allegedly refuse to pay debts, except to a consumer reporting agency or to persons meeting the requirements of section 603(f) or 604(3)1 of this Act.

(4) The advertisement for sale of any debt to coerce payment of the debt.

(5) Causing a telephone to ring or engaging any person in telephone conversation repeatedly or continuously with intent to annoy, abuse, or harass any person at the called number.

(6) Except as provided in section 804, the placement of telephone calls without meaningful disclosure of the caller's identity.

ß 807. False or misleading representations [15 USC 1962e]

A debt collector may not use any false, deceptive, or misleading representation or means in connection with the collection of any debt. Without limiting the general application of the foregoing, the following conduct is a violation of this section:

(1) The false representation or implication that the debt collector is vouched for, bonded by, or affiliated with the United States or any State, including the use of any badge, uniform, or facsimile thereof.

(2) The false representation of —

(A) the character, amount, or legal status of any debt; or

(B) any services rendered or compensation which may be lawfully received by any debt collector for the collection of a debt.

(3) The false representation or implication that any individual is an attorney or that any communication is from an attorney.

(4) The representation or implication that nonpayment of any debt will result in the arrest or imprisonment of any person or the seizure, garnishment, attachment, or sale of any property or wages of any person unless such action is law-

ful and the debt collector or creditor intends to take such action.
(5) The threat to take any action that cannot legally be taken or that is not intended to be taken.
(6) The false representation or implication that a sale, referral, or other transfer of any interest in a debt shall cause the consumer to —
(A) lose any claim or defense to payment of the debt; or
(B) become subject to any practice prohibited by this title.
(7) The false representation or implication that the consumer committed any crime or other conduct in order to disgrace the consumer.
(8) Communicating or threatening to communicate to any person credit information which is known or which should be known to be false, including the failure to communicate that a disputed debt is disputed.
(9) The use or distribution of any written communication which simulates or is falsely represented to be a document authorized, issued, or approved by any court, official, or agency of the United States or any State, or which creates a false impression as to its source, authorization, or approval.
(10) The use of any false representation or deceptive means to collect or attempt to collect any debt or to obtain information concerning a consumer.
(11) The failure to disclose in the initial written communication with the consumer and, in addition, if the initial communication with the consumer is oral, in that initial oral communication, that the debt collector is attempting to collect a debt and that any information obtained will be used for that purpose, and the failure to disclose in subsequent communications that the communication is from a debt collector, except that this paragraph shall not apply to a formal pleading made in connection with a legal action.
(12) The false representation or implication that accounts have been turned over to innocent purchasers for value.
(13) The false representation or implication that documents are legal process.
(14) The use of any business, company, or organization name other than the true name of the debt collector's business, company, or organization.
(15) The false representation or implication that documents are not legal process forms or do not require action by the consumer.
(16) The false representation or implication that a debt collector operates or is employed by a consumer reporting agency as defined by section 603(f) of this Act.
ß 808. Unfair practices [15 USC 1692f]
A debt collector may not use unfair or unconscionable means to collect or attempt to collect any debt. Without limiting the general application of the foregoing, the following conduct is a violation of this section:
(1) The collection of any amount (including any interest, fee, charge, or

expense incidental to the principal obligation) unless such amount is expressly authorized by the agreement creating the debt or permitted by law.
(2) The acceptance by a debt collector from any person of a check or other payment instrument postdated by more than five days unless such person is notified in writing of the debt collector's intent to deposit such check or instrument not more than ten nor less than three business days prior to such deposit.
(3) The solicitation by a debt collector of any postdated check or other postdated payment instrument for the purpose of threatening or instituting criminal prosecution.
(4) Depositing or threatening to deposit any postdated check or other postdated payment instrument prior to the date on such check or instrument.
(5) Causing charges to be made to any person for communications by concealment of the true propose of the communication. Such charges include, but are not limited to, collect telephone calls and telegram fees.
(6) Taking or threatening to take any nonjudicial action to effect dispossession or disablement of property if —
(A) there is no present right to possession of the property claimed as collateral through an enforceable security interest;
(B) there is no present intention to take possession of the property; or
(C) the property is exempt by law from such dispossession or disablement.
(7) Communicating with a consumer regarding a debt by post card.
(8) Using any language or symbol, other than the debt collector's address, on any envelope when communicating with a consumer by use of the mails or by telegram, except that a debt collector may use his business name if such name does not indicate that he is in the debt collection business.
ß 809. Validation of debts [15 USC 1692g]
(a) Within five days after the initial communication with a consumer in connection with the collection of any debt, a debt collector shall, unless the following information is contained in the initial communication or the consumer has paid the debt, send the consumer a written notice containing —
(1) the amount of the debt;
(2) the name of the creditor to whom the debt is owed;
(3) a statement that unless the consumer, within thirty days after receipt of the notice, disputes the validity of the debt, or any portion thereof, the debt will be assumed to be valid by the debt collector;
(4) a statement that if the consumer notifies the debt collector in writing within the thirty-day period that the debt, or any portion thereof, is disputed, the debt collector will obtain verification of the debt or a copy of a judgment against the consumer and a copy of such verification or judgment will be mailed to the con-

sumer by the debt collector; and
(5) a statement that, upon the consumer's written request within the thirty-day period, the debt collector will provide the consumer with the name and address of the original creditor, if different from the current creditor.
(b) If the consumer notifies the debt collector in writing within the thirty-day period described in subsection (a) that the debt, or any portion thereof, is disputed, or that the consumer requests the name and address of the original creditor, the debt collector shall cease collection of the debt, or any disputed portion thereof, until the debt collector obtains verification of the debt or any copy of a judgment, or the name and address of the original creditor, and a copy of such verification or judgment, or name and address of the original creditor, is mailed to the consumer by the debt collector.
(c) The failure of a consumer to dispute the validity of a debt under this section may not be construed by any court as an admission of liability by the consumer.
ß 810. Multiple debts [15 USC 1692h]
If any consumer owes multiple debts and makes any single payment to any debt collector with respect to such debts, such debt collector may not apply such payment to any debt which is disputed by the consumer and, where applicable, shall apply such payment in accordance with the consumer's directions.
ß 811. Legal actions by debt collectors [15 USC 1692i]
(a) Any debt collector who brings any legal action on a debt against any consumer shall —
(1) in the case of an action to enforce an interest in real property securing the consumer's obligation, bring such action only in a judicial district or similar legal entity in which such real property is located; or
(2) in the case of an action not described in paragraph (1), bring such action only in the judicial district or similar legal entity —
(A) in which such consumer signed the contract sued upon; or
(B) in which such consumer resides at the commencement of the action.
(b) Nothing in this title shall be construed to authorize the bringing of legal actions by debt collectors.
ß 812. Furnishing certain deceptive forms [15 USC 1692j]
(a) It is unlawful to design, compile, and furnish any form knowing that such form would be used to create the false belief in a consumer that a person other than the creditor of such consumer is participating in the collection of or in an attempt to collect a debt such consumer allegedly owes such creditor, when in fact such person is not so participating.
(b) Any person who violates this section shall be liable to the same extent and in the same manner as a debt collector is liable under section 813 for failure

to comply with a provision of this title.

ß 813. Civil liability [15 USC 1692k]

(a) Except as otherwise provided by this section, any debt collector who fails to comply with any provision of this title with respect to any person is liable to such person in an amount equal to the sum of —

(1) any actual damage sustained by such person as a result of such failure;

(2) (A) in the case of any action by an individual, such additional damages as the court may allow, but not exceeding $1,000; or

(B) in the case of a class action, (i) such amount for each named plaintiff as could be recovered under subparagraph (A), and (ii) such amount as the court may allow for all other class members, without regard to a minimum individual recovery, not to exceed the lesser of $500,000 or 1 per centum of the net worth of the debt collector; and

(3) in the case of any successful action to enforce the foregoing liability, the costs of the action, together with a reasonable attorney's fee as determined by the court. On a finding by the court that an action under this section was brought in bad faith and for the purpose of harassment, the court may award to the defendant attorney's fees reasonable in relation to the work expended and costs.

(b) In determining the amount of liability in any action under subsection (a), the court shall consider, among other relevant factors —

(1) in any individual action under subsection (a)(2)(A), the frequency and persistence of noncompliance by the debt collector, the nature of such noncompliance, and the extent to which such noncompliance was intentional; or

(2) in any class action under subsection (a)(2)(B), the frequency and persistence of noncompliance by the debt collector, the nature of such noncompliance, the resources of the debt collector, the number of persons adversely affected, and the extent to which the debt collector's noncompliance was intentional.

(c) A debt collector may not be held liable in any action brought under this title if the debt collector shows by a preponderance of evidence that the violation was not intentional and resulted from a bona fide error notwithstanding the maintenance of procedures reasonably adapted to avoid any such error.

(d) An action to enforce any liability created by this title may be brought in any appropriate United States district court without regard to the amount in controversy, or in any other court of competent jurisdiction, within one year from the date on which the violation occurs.

(e) No provision of this section imposing any liability shall apply to any act done or omitted in good faith in conformity with any advisory opinion of the Commission, notwithstanding that after such act or omission has occurred, such opinion is amended, rescinded, or determined by judicial or other authority to be invalid for any reason.

ß 814. Administrative enforcement [15 USC 1692l]

(a) Compliance with this title shall be enforced by the Commission, except to the extend that enforcement of the requirements imposed under this title is specifically committed to another agency under subsection (b). For purpose of the exercise by the Commission of its functions and powers under the Federal Trade Commission Act, a violation of this title shall be deemed an unfair or deceptive act or practice in violation of that Act. All of the functions and powers of the Commission under the Federal Trade Commission Act are available to the Commission to enforce compliance by any person with this title, irrespective of whether that person is engaged in commerce or meets any other jurisdictional tests in the Federal Trade Commission Act, including the power to enforce the provisions of this title in the same manner as if the violation had been a violation of a Federal Trade Commission trade regulation rule.

(b) Compliance with any requirements imposed under this title shall be enforced under —

(1) section 8 of the Federal Deposit Insurance Act, in the case of —

(A) national banks, by the Comptroller of the Currency;

(B) member banks of the Federal Reserve System (other than national banks), by the Federal Reserve Board; and

(C) banks the deposits or accounts of which are insured by the Federal Deposit Insurance Corporation (other than members of the Federal Reserve System), by the Board of Directors of the Federal Deposit Insurance Corporation;

(2) section 5(d) of the Home Owners Loan Act of 1933, section 407 of the National Housing Act, and sections 6(i) and 17 of the Federal Home Loan Bank Act, by the Federal Home Loan Bank Board (acting directing or through the Federal Savings and Loan Insurance Corporation), in the case of any institution subject to any of those provisions;

(3) the Federal Credit Union Act, by the Administrator of the National Credit Union Administration with respect to any Federal credit union;

(4) subtitle IV of Title 49, by the Interstate Commerce Commission with respect to any common carrier subject to such subtitle;

(5) the Federal Aviation Act of 1958, by the Secretary of Transportation with respect to any air carrier or any foreign air carrier subject to that Act; and

(6) the Packers and Stockyards Act, 1921 (except as provided in section 406 of that Act), by the Secretary of Agriculture with respect to any activities subject to that Act.

(c) For the purpose of the exercise by any agency referred to in subsection (b) of its powers under any Act referred to in that subsection, a violation of any requirement imposed under this title shall be deemed to be a violation of a requirement imposed under that Act. In addition to its powers under any provision of law specifically referred to in subsection (b), each of the agencies referred to in that subsection may exercise, for the purpose of enforcing compliance with any requirement imposed under this title any other authority conferred on it by law, except as provided in subsection (d).

(d) Neither the Commission nor any other agency referred to in subsection (b) may promulgate trade regulation rules or other regulations with respect to the collection of debts by debt collectors as defined in this title.

ß 815. Reports to Congress by the Commission [15 USC 1692m]

(a) Not later than one year after the effective date of this title and at one-year intervals thereafter, the Commission shall make reports to the Congress concerning the administration of its functions under this title, including such recommendations as the Commission deems necessary or appropriate. In addition, each report of the Commission shall include its assessment of the extent to which compliance with this title is being achieved and a summary of the enforcement actions taken by the Commission under section 814 of this title.

(b) In the exercise of its functions under this title, the Commission may obtain upon request the views of any other Federal agency which exercises enforcement functions under section 814 of this title.

ß 816. Relation to State laws [15 USC 1692n]

This title does not annul, alter, or affect, or exempt any person subject to the provisions of this title from complying with the laws of any State with respect to debt collection practices, except to the extent that those laws are inconsistent with any provision of this title, and then only to the extent of the inconsistency. For purposes of this section, a State law is not inconsistent with this title if the protection such law affords any consumer is greater than the protection provided by this title.

ß 817. Exemption for State regulation [15 USC 1692o]

The Commission shall by regulation exempt from the requirements of this title any class of debt collection practices within any State if the Commission determines that under the law of that State that class of debt collection practices is subject to requirements substantially similar to those imposed by this title, and that there is adequate provision for enforcement.

ß 818. Effective date [15 USC 1692 note]

This title takes effect upon the expiration of six months after the date of its enactment, but section 809 shall apply only with respect to debts for which the initial attempt to collect occurs after such effective date.

Approved September 20, 1977

ENDNOTES
1. So in original; however, should read "604(a)(3)."

LEGISLATIVE HISTORY:
Public Law 95-109 [H.R. 5294]
HOUSE REPORT No. 95-131 (Comm. on Banking, Finance, and Urban Affairs).
SENATE REPORT No. 95-382 (Comm. on Banking, Housing, and Urban Affairs).
CONGRESSIONAL RECORD, Vol. 123 (1977):
Apr. 4, considered and passed House.
Aug. 5, considered and passed Senate, amended.
Sept. 8, House agreed to Senate amendment.
WEEKLY COMPILATION OF PRESIDENTIAL DOCUMENTS, Vol. 13, No. 39:
Sept. 20, Presidential statement.
AMENDMENTS:
SECTION 621, SUBSECTIONS (b)(3), (b)(4) and (b)(5) were amended to transfer certain administrative enforcement responsibilities, pursuant to Pub. L. 95-473, ß 3(b), Oct. 17, 1978. 92 Stat. 166; Pub. L. 95-630, Title V. ß 501, November 10, 1978, 92 Stat. 3680; Pub. L. 98-443, ß 9(h), Oct. 4, 1984, 98 Stat. 708.
SECTION 803, SUBSECTION (6), defining "debt collector," was amended to repeal the attorney at law exemption at former Section (6)(F) and to redesignate Section 803(6)(G) pursuant to Pub. L. 99-361, July 9, 1986, 100 Stat. 768. For legislative history, see H.R. 237, HOUSE REPORT No. 99-405 (Comm. on Banking, Finance and Urban Affairs). CONGRESSIONAL RECORD: Vol. 131 (1985): Dec. 2, considered and passed House. Vol. 132 (1986): June 26, considered and passed Senate.
SECTION 807, SUBSECTION (11), was amended to affect when debt collectors must state (a) that they are attempting to collect a debt and (b) that information obtained will be used for that purpose, pursuant to Pub. L. 104-208 ß 2305, 110 Stat. 3009 (Sept. 30, 1996).

CHAPTER 2—CREDIT REPAIR ORGANIZATIONS(1)
SEC. 2451. REGULATION OF CREDIT REPAIR ORGANIZATIONS.
Title IV of the Consumer Credit Protection Act (Public Law 90-321, 82 Stat. 164) is amended to read as follows:
TITLE IV—CREDIT REPAIR ORGANIZATIONS"

SEC. 401. SHORT TITLE.(2)

This title may be cited as the 'Credit Repair Organizations Act'.

SEC. 402. FINDINGS AND PURPOSES.(3)

(a) Findings.—The Congress makes the following findings:

(1) Consumers have a vital interest in establishing and maintaining their credit worthiness and credit standing in order to obtain and use credit. As a result, consumers who have experienced credit problems may seek assistance from credit repair organizations which offer to improve the credit standing of such consumers.

(2) Certain advertising and business practices of some companies engaged in the business of credit repair services have worked a financial hardship upon consumers, particularly those of limited economic means and who are inexperienced in credit matters.

(b) Purposes.—The purposes of this title are—

(1) to ensure that prospective buyers of the services of credit repair organizations are provided with the information necessary to make an informed decision regarding the purchase of such services; and

(2) to protect the public from unfair or deceptive advertising and business practices by credit repair organizations.

SEC. 403. DEFINITIONS.(4)

For purposes of this title, the following definitions apply:

(1) Consumer. — The term 'consumer' means an individual.

(2) Consumer credit transaction. — The term 'consumer credit transaction' means any transaction in which credit is offered or extended to an individual for personal, family, or household purposes.

(3) Credit repair organization. — The term 'credit repair organization'—

(A) means any person who uses any instrumentality of interstate commerce or the mails to sell, provide, or perform (or represent that such person can or will sell, provide, or perform) any service, in return for the payment of money or other valuable consideration, for the express or implied purpose of—

(i) improving any consumer's credit record, credit history, or credit rating; or
(ii) providing advice or assistance to any consumer with regard to any activity or service described in clause (i); and
(B) does not include—

(i) any nonprofit organization which is exempt from taxation under section 501(c)(3) of the Internal Revenue Code of 1986;
(ii) any creditor (as defined in section 103 of the Truth in Lending Act),(5) with respect to any consumer, to the extent the creditor is assisting the consumer to restructure any debt owed by the consumer to the creditor; or
(iii) any depository institution (as that term is defined in section 3 of the Federal Deposit Insurance Act) or any Federal or State credit union (as those terms are defined in section 101 of the Federal Credit Union Act), or any affiliate or subsidiary of such a depository institution or credit union.
(4) Credit.—The term 'credit' has the meaning given to such term in section 103(e) of this Act.(6)
SEC. 404. PROHIBITED PRACTICES.(7)
(a) In General.—No person may—
(1) make any statement, or counsel or advise any consumer to make any statement, which is untrue or misleading (or which, upon the exercise of reasonable care, should be known by the credit repair organization, officer, employee, agent, or other person to be untrue or misleading) with respect to any consumer's credit worthiness, credit standing, or credit capacity to—

(A) any consumer reporting agency (as defined in section 603(f) of this Act);(8) or
(B) any person—

(i) who has extended credit to the consumer; or
(ii) to whom the consumer has applied or is applying for an extension of credit;
(2) make any statement, or counsel or advise any consumer to make any statement, the intended effect of which is to alter the consumer's identification to prevent the display of the consumer's credit record, history, or rating for the purpose of concealing adverse information that is accurate and not obsolete

to—

(A) any consumer reporting agency;
(B) any person—

(i) who has extended credit to the consumer; or
(ii) to whom the consumer has applied or is applying for an extension of credit;
(3) make or use any untrue or misleading representation of the services of the credit repair organization; or
(4) engage, directly or indirectly, in any act, practice, or course of business that constitutes or results in the commission of, or an attempt to commit, a fraud or deception on any person in connection with the offer or sale of the services of the credit repair organization.
(b) Payment in Advance.—No credit repair organization may charge or receive any money or other valuable consideration for the performance of any service which the credit repair organization has agreed to perform for any consumer before such service is fully performed.
SEC. 405. DISCLOSURES.(9)
(a) Disclosure Required.—Any credit repair organization shall provide any consumer with the following written statement before any contract or agreement between the consumer and the credit repair organization is executed:
'Consumer Credit File Rights Under State and Federal Law
You have a right to dispute inaccurate information in your credit report by contacting the credit bureau directly. However, neither you nor any "credit repair" company or credit repair organization has the right to have accurate, current, and verifiable information removed from your credit report. The credit bureau must remove accurate, negative information from your report only if it is over 7 years old. Bankruptcy information can be reported for 10 years.
You have a right to obtain a copy of your credit report from a credit bureau. You may be charged a reasonable fee. There is no fee, however, if you have been turned down for credit, employment, insurance, or a rental dwelling because of information in your credit report within the preceding 60 days. The credit bureau must provide someone to help you interpret the information in your credit file. You are entitled to receive a free copy of your credit report if you are unemployed and intend to apply for employment in the next 60 days, if you are a recipient of public welfare assistance, or if you have reason to believe that there is inaccurate information in your credit report due to fraud.
You have a right to sue a credit repair organization that violates the Credit Repair Organization Act. This law prohibits deceptive practices by credit repair

organizations.

You have the right to cancel your contract with any credit repair organization for any reason within 3 business days from the date you signed it.

Credit bureaus are required to follow reasonable procedures to ensure that the information they report is accurate. However, mistakes may occur.

You may, on your own, notify a credit bureau in writing that you dispute the accuracy of information in your credit file. The credit bureau must then reinvestigate and modify or remove inaccurate or incomplete information. The credit bureau may not charge any fee for this service. Any pertinent information and copies of all documents you have concerning an error should be given to the credit bureau.

If the credit bureau's reinvestigation does not resolve the dispute to your satisfaction, you may send a brief statement to the credit bureau, to be kept in your file, explaining why you think the record is inaccurate. The credit bureau must include a summary of your statement about disputed information with any report it issues about you.

The Federal Trade Commission regulates credit bureaus and credit repair organizations. For more information contact:

The Public Reference Branch
Federal Trade Commission
Washington, D.C. 20580'.

(b) Separate Statement Requirement.—The written statement required under this section shall be provided as a document which is separate from any written contract or other agreement between the credit repair organization and the consumer or any other written material provided to the consumer.

(c) Retention of Compliance Records.—

(1) In general.—The credit repair organization shall maintain a copy of the statement signed by the consumer acknowledging receipt of the statement.

(2) Maintenance for 2 years.—The copy of any consumer's statement shall be maintained in the organization's files for 2 years after the date on which the statement is signed by the consumer.

SEC. 406. CREDIT REPAIR ORGANIZATIONS CONTRACTS.(10)

(a) Written Contracts Required.—No services may be provided by any credit repair organization for any consumer—

(1) unless a written and dated contract (for the purchase of such services) which meets the requirements of subsection (b) has been signed by the consumer; or

(2) before the end of the 3-business-day period beginning on the date the contract is signed.

(b) Terms and Conditions of Contract.—No contract referred to in subsection

(a) meets the requirements of this subsection unless such contract includes (in writing)—
(1) the terms and conditions of payment, including the total amount of all payments to be made by the consumer to the credit repair organization or to any other person;
(2) a full and detailed description of the services to be performed by the credit repair organization for the consumer, including—

(A) all guarantees of performance; and
(B) an estimate of—

(i) the date by which the performance of the services (to be performed by the credit repair organization or any other person) will be complete; or
(ii) the length of the period necessary to perform such services;
(3) the credit repair organization's name and principal business address; and
(4) a conspicuous statement in bold face type, in immediate proximity to the space reserved for the consumer's signature on the contract, which reads as follows: 'You may cancel this contract without penalty or obligation at any time before midnight of the 3rd business day after the date on which you signed the contract. See the attached notice of cancellation form for an explanation of this right.'.
SEC. 407. RIGHT TO CANCEL CONTRACT.(11)
(a) In General. — Any consumer may cancel any contract with any credit repair organization without penalty or obligation by notifying the credit repair organization of the consumer's intention to do so at any time before midnight of the 3rd business day which begins after the date on which the contract or agreement between the consumer and the credit repair organization is executed or would, but for this subsection, become enforceable against the parties.
(b) Cancellation Form and Other Information. — Each contract shall be accompanied by a form, in duplicate, which has the heading 'Notice of Cancellation' and contains in bold face type the following statement:
'You may cancel this contract, without any penalty or obligation, at any time before midnight of the 3rd day which begins after the date the contract is signed by you.
To cancel this contract, mail or deliver a signed, dated copy of this cancellation notice, or any other written notice to (name of credit repair organization) at (address of credit repair organization) before midnight on (date)
I hereby cancel this transaction,
(date)
(purchaser's signature).'.

(c) Consumer Copy of Contract Required.—Any consumer who enters into any contract with any credit repair organization shall be given, by the organization—

(1) a copy of the completed contract and the disclosure statement required under section 405; and

(2) a copy of any other document the credit repair organization requires the consumer to sign, at the time the contract or the other document is signed.

SEC. 408. NONCOMPLIANCE WITH THIS TITLE.(12)

(a) Consumer Waivers Invalid.—Any waiver by any consumer of any protection provided by or any right of the consumer under this title—

(1) shall be treated as void; and

(2) may not be enforced by any Federal or State court or any other person.

(b) Attempt To Obtain Waiver.—Any attempt by any person to obtain a waiver from any consumer of any protection provided by or any right of the consumer under this title shall be treated as a violation of this title.

(c) Contracts Not in Compliance.—Any contract for services which does not comply with the applicable provisions of this title—

(1) shall be treated as void; and

(2) may not be enforced by any Federal or State court or any other person.

SEC. 409. CIVIL LIABILITY.(13)

(a) Liability Established.—Any person who fails to comply with any provision of this title with respect to any other person shall be liable to such person in an amount equal to the sum of the amounts determined under each of the following paragraphs:

(1) Actual damages.—The greater of—

(A) the amount of any actual damage sustained by such person as a result of such failure; or

(B) any amount paid by the person to the credit repair organization.

(2) Punitive damages.—

(A) Individual actions.—In the case of any action by an individual, such additional amount as the court may allow.

(B) Class actions.—In the case of a class action, the sum of—

(i) the aggregate of the amount which the court may allow for each named plaintiff; and

(ii) the aggregate of the amount which the court may allow for each other class member, without regard to any minimum individual recovery.

(3) Attorneys' fees.—In the case of any successful action to enforce any liabil-

ity under paragraph (1) or (2), the costs of the action, together with reasonable attorneys' fees.

(b) Factors to Be Considered in Awarding Punitive Damages.—In determining the amount of any liability of any credit repair organization under subsection (a)(2), the court shall consider, among other relevant factors—

(1) the frequency and persistence of noncompliance by the credit repair organization;

(2) the nature of the noncompliance;

(3) the extent to which such noncompliance was intentional; and

(4) in the case of any class action, the number of consumers adversely affected.

SEC. 410. ADMINISTRATIVE ENFORCEMENT.(14)

(a) In General.—Compliance with the requirements imposed under this title with respect to credit repair organizations shall be enforced under the Federal Trade Commission Act by the Federal Trade Commission.

(b) Violations of This Title Treated as Violations of Federal Trade Commission Act.—

(1) In general. — For the purpose of the exercise by the Federal Trade Commission of the Commission's functions and powers under the Federal Trade Commission Act, any violation of any requirement or prohibition imposed under this title with respect to credit repair organizations shall constitute an unfair or deceptive act or practice in commerce in violation of section 5(a) of the Federal Trade Commission Act.

(2) Enforcement authority under other law. — All functions and powers of the Federal Trade Commission under the Federal Trade Commission Act shall be available to the Commission to enforce compliance with this title by any person subject to enforcement by the Federal Trade Commission pursuant to this subsection, including the power to enforce the provisions of this title in the same manner as if the violation had been a violation of any Federal Trade Commission trade regulation rule, without regard to whether the credit repair organization—

(A) is engaged in commerce; or

(B) meets any other jurisdictional tests in the Federal Trade Commission Act.

(c) State Action for Violations.—

(1) Authority of states. — In addition to such other remedies as are provided under State law, whenever the chief law enforcement officer of a State, or an official or agency designated by a State, has reason to believe that any person has violated or is violating this title, the State—

(A) may bring an action to enjoin such violation;
(B) may bring an action on behalf of its residents to recover damages for which the person is liable to such residents under section 409 as a result of the violation; and
(C) in the case of any successful action under subparagraph (A) or (B), shall be awarded the costs of the action and reasonable attorney fees as determined by the court.
(2) Rights of commission.—

(A) Notice to commission.—The State shall serve prior written notice of any civil action under paragraph (1) upon the Federal Trade Commission and provide the Commission with a copy of its complaint, except in any case where such prior notice is not feasible, in which case the State shall serve such notice immediately upon instituting such action.
(B) Intervention.—The Commission shall have the right—

(i) to intervene in any action referred to in subparagraph (A);
(ii) upon so intervening, to be heard on all matters arising in the action; and
(iii) to file petitions for appeal.
(3) Investigatory powers. — For purposes of bringing any action under this subsection, nothing in this subsection shall prevent the chief law enforcement officer, or an official or agency designated by a State, from exercising the powers conferred on the chief law enforcement officer or such official by the laws of such State to conduct investigations or to administer oaths or affirmations or to compel the attendance of witnesses or the production of documentary and other evidence.
(4) Limitation. — Whenever the Federal Trade Commission has instituted a civil action for violation of this title, no State may, during the pendency of such action, bring an action under this section against any defendant named in the complaint of the Commission for any violation of this title that is alleged in that complaint.
SEC. 411. STATUTE OF LIMITATIONS.(15)
Any action to enforce any liability under this title may be brought before the later of—
(1) the end of the 5-year period beginning on the date of the occurrence of the violation involved; or
(2) in any case in which any credit repair organization has materially and willfully misrepresented any information which—

(A) the credit repair organization is required, by any provision of this title, to

disclose to any consumer; and
(B) is material to the establishment of the credit repair organization's liability to the consumer under this title, the end of the 5-year period beginning on the date of the discovery by the consumer of the misrepresentation.

SEC. 412. RELATION TO STATE LAW.(16)

This title shall not annul, alter, affect, or exempt any person subject to the provisions of this title from complying with any law of any State except to the extent that such law is inconsistent with any provision of this title, and then only to the extent of the inconsistency.

SEC. 413. EFFECTIVE DATE.(17)

This title shall apply after the end of the 6-month period beginning on the date of the enactment of the Credit Repair Organizations Act,(18) except with respect to contracts entered into by a credit repair organization before the end of such period.".

1. Pub. L. No. 104-208, 110 Stat. 3009 (Sept. 30, 1996). The amendments to the credit statutes are in Title II of the Act, entitled "Economic Growth and Regulatory Paperwork Reduction." The footnotes in this copy of the Act are not part of the Act, but are cross-references inserted by the FTC staff for the convenience of the reader.
2. To be codified as 15 U.S.C. ß 1679.
3. To be codified as 15 U.S.C. ß 1679a.
4. To be codified as 15 U.S.C. ß 1679b.
5. Truth in Lending Act ß 103(f) states in pertinent part: "The term 'creditor' refers only to creditros who regularly extend, or arrange for the extension of, credit which is payable by agreement in more than four installments or for which the payment of a finance charge is or may be required, whether in connection with loans, sales pf property or services, or otherwise. . . ."
6. TILA ß 103(e) states: "The term 'credit' means the right granted by a creditor to a debtor to defer payment of debt or to incur debt and defer its payment."
7. To be codified as 15 U.S.C. ß 1679c.
8. Fair Credit Reporting Act (FCRA) ß 603(f) states: "The term 'consumer reporting agency' means any person which, for monetary fees, dues, or on a cooperative nonprofit basis, regularly engages in whole or in part in the practice of assembling or evaluating consumer credit information or other information on consumers for the purpose of furnishing consumer reports to third parties, and which uses any means or facility of interstate commerce for the purpose of preparing or furnishing consumer reports."
9. To be codified as 15 U.S.C. ß 1679d.
10. To be codified as 15 U.S.C. ß 1679e.

11. To be codified as 15 U.S.C. ß 1679f.
12. To be codified as 15 U.S.C. ß 1679g.
13. To be codified as 15 U.S.C. ß 1679h.
14. To be codified as 15 U.S.C. ß 1679i.
15. To be codified as 15 U.S.C. ß 1679j.
16. To be codified as 15 U.S.C. ß 1679k.
17. To be codified as 15 U.S.C. ß 1679l.
18. The statute was signed by the President on September 30, 1996.

INSTANT CREDIT REPAIR KIT

Appendix D State Attorney Generals

Your state attorney general can be a consumer's best friend, especially in the area of credit issues. Your state's attorney general can advise you on how to proceed in all matters of law , tell you what paperwork you need, help you find affordable representation, give you statutes, cite legal precedences pertaining to your state, help you get in touch with the consumer protection agency. In fact, in many states, the attorney general shares his/her office with the state consumer protection agency.

Here are the current state-by-state attorney general offices and their contact information:

State	Attorney General	Phone
* Alabama	Bill Pryor	(334) 2427300

State House, 11 S. Union Street, Montgomery, AL 36130
http://www.ago.state.al.us

State	Attorney General	Phone
* Alaska	Greg Renkes	(907) 465-3500

P.O. Box 110300, Diamond Courthouse, Juneau, AK 99811-0300
http://www.law.state.ak.us

* Arizona Janet Napolitano (602) 542-4266
1275 W. Washington Street, Phoeniz, AZ 85007
http://www.attorneygeneralstat.state.az.us

* Arkansas Mark Lunsford Pryor (800) 482-8982
200 Tower Building, 323 Center Street, Little Rock AR 72201-2610
http://www.ag,state.ar.us

* California Bill Lockyer (916) 445-9555
1300 I Ste. 1740, Sacramento, CA 95814
http://www.caag.state.ca.us

* Colorado Ken Salazar ((303 866-4500
Dept. of Law, 1525 Sherman St., Denver, CO 80203
http://www.ago.state.co.us

* Connecticut Richard Blumenthal (*860) 808-5318
55 Elm Street, Hartford, CT 06141-0120
http://www.cslib.org/attygenl/

* Delaware M. Jane Brady (302) 577-8338
Carvel Street Office Bldg., 820 N. French St., Wilmington, DE 19801
http://www.state.de.us/attgen

* District of Columbia Arabella W. Teal (202) 724-1305
Office of the Corporation Counsel, 441 4th St., NW, Washington, DC 20001
http://occ.dc.gov/

* Florida Richard Doran (850) 487-1963
The Capitol, PL 01, Tallahassee, FL 32399-1050
http://legal.firm.edu

* Georgia Thurbert E. Baker (404) 656-3300
40 Capitol Square, SW, Atlanta, GA 30334-1300
http://ganet.org/ago/

* Hawaii Thomas R. Keller (671) 475-3409
425 Queen Street, Honolulu, HI 96813
http://www.state.hi.us/ag/index.html

* Idaho Allan G. Lance (208) 334-2400
Statehouse, Boise, ID 83720-1000
http://www2.state.id.us/ag/

* Illinois Jim Ryan (312) 854-2503
James R. Thompson Ctr., 100 W. Randolph St., Chicago, IL 60601
http://www.ag.state.il.us

* Indiana Steve Carter ((317) 232-6201
Indiana Government Center South - 5th Floor, 402 W. Washington St., Indianapolis, IN 46204
http://www.in.gov/attorneygeneral/

* Iowa Tom Miller (515) 281-5164
Hoover State Office Bldg., 1305 E. Walnut, Des Moines, IA 50319
http://www.IowaAttorneyGeneral.org

* Kansas Carla J. Stovall (785) 296-2215
120 S.W. 10th Ave., 2nd Floor, Topeka, KS 66612-1597
http://www.ink.org/public/ksag

* Kentucky Albert Benjamin Chandler III (502) 696-5300
State Capitol, Rm. 116, Frankfort, KY 40601
http://www.law.state.ky.us

* Louisiana Richard O. Leyoub (225) 342-7013
Dept. of Justice, P.O. Box 94095, Baton Rouge, LA 70804-4095
http://www.ag.state.la.us/

* Maine G. Steven Rowe (207) 626-8800
State House Station 6, Augusta, ME 04333
http://www.state.me.us/ag

* Maryland J. Joseph Curran Jr. (410) 576-6300
200 St. Paul Place, Baltimore, MD 21202-2202
http://www.oag.state.md.us

* Massachusetts Tom Reilly (617) 727-2200

1 Ashburton Place, Boston MA 02108-1698
http://www.ago.state.ma.us

* Michigan — Jennifer Granholm — (517) 373-1110
P.O. Box 30212, 525 W. Ottawa St., Lansing, MI 48909-0212
http://www.ag.state.mi.us

* Minnesota — Mike Hatch — (651) 296-3353
State Capitol, Ste. 102, St. Paul, MN 55155
http://www.ag.state.mn.us

* Mississippi — Mike Moore — (601) 359-3680
Dept. of Justice, P.O. Box 220, Jackson, MS 39205-0220
http://www.ago.state.ms.us

* Missouri — Jeremiah W. Nixon — (573) 751-3321
Supreme Ct. Bldg. 207 W. High Street, Jefferson City, MO 65101
http://www.ago.state.mo.us

* Montana — Mike McGrath — (406) 444-2026
Justice Bldg., 215 N. Sanders, Helena, MT 59620-1401
http://doj.state.mt.us/

* Nebraska — Don Stenberg — (402) 471-2682
State Capitol, P.O. Box 98920, Lincoln, NE 68509-8920
http://www.nol.org/home/ago

* Nevada — Frankie Sue Del Papa — (775) 684-1100
Old Supreme Ct. Bldg, 100 N. Carson St., Carson City, NV 89701
http://ag.state.nv.us/

* New Hampshire — Philip T. McLaughlin — (603) 271-3658
State House Annex, 25 Capitol St., Concord, NH 03301-6397
http://www.state.nh.us/nhdoj

* New Jersey — David Samson — (609) 292-8740
Richard J. Hughes Justice Complex, 25 Market Street, CN 060, Trenton, NJ 08625
http://www.state.nj.us/lps/

* New Mexico Patricia A. Madrid (505) 827-6000
P.O. Drawer 1508, Santa Fe, NM 87504-1508
http://www.ago.state.nm.us

* New York Elliot Spitzer (518) 474-7330
Dept. of Law - The Capitol, 2nd FL, Albany, NY 12224
http://www.oag.state.ny.us

* North Carolina Roy Cooper (919) 716-6400
Dept. of Justice, P.O. Box629, Raleigh, NC 27602-0629
http://www.jus.state.nc.us

* North Dakota Wayne Stenehjem (701) 328-2210
State Capitol, 600 E. Boulevard Ave., Bismarck, ND 58505-0040
http://www.ag.state.nd.us

* Ohio Betty D. Montgomery (614) 466-4320
State Office Tower, 30 E. Broad St., Columbus, OH 43266-0410
http://www.ag.state.oh.us

* Oklahoma W.A. Drew Edmondson (405) 521-3921
State Capitol, Rm, 112, 2300 N. Lincoln Blvd., Oklahoma City, OK 73105
http://www.oag.state.ok.us

* Oregon Hardy Myers (503) 378-4732
Justice Building, 1162 Court Street, NE, Salem, OR 97301
http://www.doj.state.or.us

* Pennsylvania Mike Fisher (717) 787-3391
Strawberry Square, Harrisburg, PA 17120
http://www.attorneygeneral.gov

* Rhode Island Sheldon Whitehouse (401) 274-4400
150 S. Main Street, Providence, RI 02903
http://www.justica.gobiermo.pr

* South Carolina Charlie Condon (803) 734-4399
Rembert C. Dennis Office Bldg., P.O. Box 11549, Columbia, SC 29211-1549
http://www.riag.state.ri.us

* South Dakota Mike Barnett (605) 773-3215
500 E Capitol, Pierre, SD 57501-5070
http://www.state.sd.us/attorney/attorney.html

* Tennessee Paul G. Summers (615) 741-5860
500 Charlotte Ave., Nashville, TN 37243
http://www.attorneygeneral.state.tn.us

* Texas Greg Abbott (512) 463-2100
Capitol Station, P.O. Box 12548, Austin, TX 78711-2548
http://www.oag.state.tx.us

* Utah Mark Shurtleff (801) 538-9600
State Capitol, Rm. 236, Salt Lake City, UT 84114-0810
http://www.attorneygeneral.utah.gov/

* Vermont William H. Sorrell (802) 828-3173
100 State St., Montpelier, VT 05609-1001
http://www.state.vt.us.atg

* Virginia Jerry Kilgore (804) 786-2071
900 E. Main St., Richmond, VA 23219
http://www.oag.state.va.us

* Washington Christine O. Gregoire (360) 753-6200
P.O. Box 40100, 1125 Washington St., SE, Olympia, WA 98504-0100
http://www.wa.gov/ago

* West Virginia Darrell Vivian McGraw Jr. (304) 558-2021
State Capitol, 1900 Kanawha Blvd., E. Charleston, WV 25305
http://www.state.wv.us/wvag

* Wisconsin James E. Doyle (608) 266-1221
State Capitol, Ste. 114 E, P.O. Box 7857, Madison, WI 53707-7857
http://www.doj.state.wi.us

* Wyoming Hoke MacMillan (307) 777-7841
State Capitol Bldg., Cheyenne, WY 82002
http://attorneygeneral.state.wy.us

CREDIT REPAIR WORKBOOK

Glossary

* Annual Fee: A once-a-year charged levied by many credit card companies. This fee is in addition to the interest charged on purchases and cash advances.

* Annual Percentage Rate (APR): The cost of credit expressed as a yearly rate.

* Balance: The total amount owed on a credit account.

* Bankruptcy: Legally declared unable to pay debts as they come due. Bankruptcy can severely impact the ability to borrow money.

* Billing Error: Any mistake in your monthly statement as defined by the Fair Credit Billing Act.

* Budget: An itemized list of all expenses.

* Charge-Offs: These are loans or debts that have gone unpaid by the creditor. The creditor "gives up" on collecting payment and reports the charge-off to the credit bureau for inclusion on an individual's credit report. Most lenders, however, consider charge-offs as debts that are still owed.

* Collection Agency: A company that collects debts on behalf of creditors.

* Consumer Credit Counseling: A service that assists consumers in combining debts into one monthly payment.

* Credit: The right granted by a creditor to pay in the future to buy or borrow in

the present.

* Credit Bureau: An agency that keeps your credit record; also called a credit-reporting agency (CRA).

* Credit Card: Any card, plate, or coupon book used periodically or repeatedly to borrow money or buy goods or services on credit.

* Credit History: The record of how you've borrowed and repaid your debts.

* Creditor: A person or business from whom you borrow or to whom you owe money.

* Credit Limit: The total amount a consumer is authorized to charge on a credit card.

* Credit Repair Companies: Private, for-profit businesses that that claim to offer consumers with credit and debt repayment problems assistance in "fixing" these problems and/ or "fixing" a negative credit report.

* Credit Report: A file maintained by a credit bureau that contains information about a person, such as where he/she works and lives, information from creditors regarding money borrowed and payments made, as well as public record information, such as whether the person has filed for bankruptcy.

* Credit Scoring System: A statistical system used to rate credit applicants according to various characteristics relevant to creditworthiness. Creditors use such a system to help them determine whether or not to give you credit.

* Creditworthiness: A person's past, present and future ability to repay debts.

* Credit Reporting Agency: An agency that keeps your credit record; also called a credit-reporting agency, or credit bureau.

* Debit Card: A plastic card, which looks similar to a credit card. Consumers may use such a card at an ATM or to make purchases, withdrawals, or other types of electronic funds transfers.

* Default: Failure to repay a loan or otherwise meet the terms of your credit agreement.

* Finance Charge: The total dollar amount credit will cost.

* Inquiry: A request for a copy of a credit report. An inquiry occurs whenever a credit application is completed and when more credit is requested. In some instances, too many inquiries on a credit report can result in a lower credit score.

* Interest: The amount charged to borrow money. It's the amount the lender charges to borrow money, and usually is expressed as a percentage of the amount borrowed.

* Judgment: Formal court orders displayed on a credit report if a debt or loan obligation is unpaid.

* Late Payments: Loan or credit payments that do not reach the lender or creditor on or before the payment due date. The listing of late payments on a credit report is very damaging to an individual's credit report.

* Minimum Payment: The smallest amount that can be paid to keep a credit account current.

* Negotiation: The process of working out a dispute with a creditor to a mutually satisfactory solution.

* Public Record Information: Information on events that are a matter of public record (courthouse records) related to creditworthiness, such as bankruptcies, foreclosures and tax liens. The presence of such information on a credit report is viewed negatively by the credit industry.

* Revolving Credit: A type of credit account in which the consumer has the option to pay the debt in full each month or make a minimum monthly payment based upon the outstanding balance.

* Secured Credit Card: A credit card backed by collateral, usually cash in the form of a bank deposit account.

* Secured Loan: A loan backed by collateral and secured against something tangible, such as a home or real estate.

* Settlement: An agreement between a debtor and a creditor that solves or eliminates a dispute.

* Truth-In-Lending: A law that requires lenders to disclose terms and costs of all loan plans, including interest rates, the APR, points and fees; payment due date and terms and late payment fees.

* Unsecured Loan: A loan in which the creditor does not hold a security interest in an item owned by the debtor. Most credit cards are unsecured.